Bible Interpretations
Twelfth Series
April 1-June 24, 1894

Genesis, Exodus, Proverbs

Bible Interpretations

Twelfth Series

Genesis, Exodus, Proverbs

These Bible Interpretations were published in the Inter-Ocean Newspaper in Chicago, Illinois during the late eighteen nineties.

.

By
Emma Curtis Hopkins

President of the Emma Curtis Hopkins Theological Seminary at Chicago, Illinois

WISEWOMAN PRESS

Bible Interpretations: Twelfth Series

By Emma Curtis Hopkins

© WiseWoman Press 2011

Managing Editor: Michael Terranova

ISBN: 978-0945385-62-2

WiseWoman Press

Vancouver, WA 98665

www.wisewomanpress.com

www.emmacurtishopkins.com

CONTENTS

	Foreword by Rev. Natalie R. Jean	ix
	Introduction by Rev. Michael Terranova	xi
I.	Jacob's Prevailing Prayer	1
	Genesis 32:9-12 Genesis 24:30	
II.	Discord In Jacob's Family	9
	Genesis 37:1-11	
III.	Joseph Sold Into Egypt	17
	Genesis 37:23-36	
IV.	Object Lessons Presented In The Book Of Genesis	25
	Genesis 41:38-48	
V.	"With Thee Is Fullness Of Joy"	33
	Genesis 45:1-15	
VI.	Change Of Heart	41
	Genesis 50:14-26	
VII.	Israel in Egypt	49
	Exodus 1:1-14	
VIII.	The Childhood of Moses	55
	Exodus 2:1-10	
IX.	Moses Sent As A Deliverer	61
	Exodus 3:10-20	
X.	The Passover Instituted	69
	Exodus 12:1-14	
XI.	Passage of the Red Sea	75
	Exodus 14:19-29	
XII.	The Woes Of The Drunkard	83
	Proverbs 23:29-35	
XIII.	REVIEW	90
	List of Bible Interpretation Series	100

Editors Note

All lessons starting with the Seventh Series of Bible Interpretations will be Sunday postings from the Inter-Ocean Newspaper in Chicago, Illinois. Many of the lessons in the following series were retrieved from the International New Thought Association Archives, in Mesa, Arizona by, Rev Joanna Rogers. Many others were retrieved from libraries in Chicago, and the Library of Congress, by Rev. Natalie Jean.

All the lessons follow the Sunday School Lesson Plan published in "Peloubet's International Sunday School Lessons". The passages to be studied are selected by an International Committee of traditional Bible Scholars.

Some of the Emma's lessons don't have a title. In these cases the heading will say "Comments and Explanations of the Golden Text," followed by the Bible passages to be studied.

Foreword

By Rev. Natalie R. Jean

I have read many teachings by Emma Curtis Hopkins, but the teachings that touch the very essence of my soul are her Bible Interpretations. There are many books written on the teachings of the Bible, but none can touch the surface of the true messages more than these Bible interpretations. With each word you can feel and see how Spirit spoke through Emma. The mystical interpretations take you on a wonderful journey to Self Realization.

Each passage opens your consciousness to a new awareness of the realities of life. The illusions of life seem to disappear through each interpretation. Emma teaches that we are the key that unlocks the doorway to the light that shines within. She incorporates ideals of other religions into her teachings, in order to understand the commonalities, so that there is a complete understanding of our Oneness. Emma opens our eyes and mind to a better today and exciting future.

Emma Curtis Hopkins, one of the Founders of New Thought teaches us to love ourselves, to speak our Truth, and to focus on our Good. My life has moved in wonderful directions because of her teachings. I know the only thing that can move me in this world is God. May these interpretations guide you to a similar path and may you truly remember that "There Is Good For You and You Ought to Have It."

Introduction

Emma Curtis Hopkins was born in 1849 in Killingsly, Connecticut. She passed on April 8, 1925. Mrs. Hopkins had a marvelous education and could read many of the worlds classical texts in their original language. During her extensive studies she was always able to discover the Universal Truths in each of the world's sacred traditions. She quotes from many of these teachings in her writings. As she was a very private person, we know little about her personal life. What we do know has been gleaned from other people or from the archived writings we have been able to discover.

Emma Curtis Hopkins was one of the greatest influences on the New Thought movement in the United States. She taught over 50,000 people the Universal Truth of knowing "God is All there is." She taught many of founders of early New Thought, and in turn these individuals expanded the influence of her teachings. All of her writings encourage the student to enter into a personal relationship with God. She presses us to deny anything except the Truth of this spiritual Presence in every area of our lives. This is the central focus of all her teachings.

The first six series of Bible Interpretations were presented at her seminary in Chicago, Illinois. The remaining Series', probably close to thirty, were printed in the Inter Ocean Newspaper in Chicago. Many of the lessons are no longer available for various reasons. It is the intention of WiseWoman Press to publish as many of these Bible Interpretations as possible. Our hope is that any missing lessons will be found or directed to us.

I am very honored to join the long line of people that have been involved in publishing Emma Curtis Hopkins's Bible Interpretations. Some confusion exists as to the numbering sequence of the lessons. In the early 1920's many of the lessons were published by the Highwatch Fellowship. Inadvertently the first two lessons were omitted from the numbering system. Rev. Joanna Rogers has corrected this mistake by finding the first two lessons and restoring them to their rightful place in the order. Rev. Rogers has been able to find many of the missing lessons at the International New Thought Alliance archives in Mesa, Arizona. Rev. Rogers painstakingly scoured the archives for the missing lessons as well as for Mrs. Hopkins other works. She has published much of what was discovered. WiseWoman Press is now publishing the correctly numbered series of the Bible Interpretations.

In the early 1940's, there was a resurgence of interest in Emma's works. At that time, Highwatch Fellowship began to publish many of her writings, and it was then that *High Mysticism*, her seminal work was published. Previously, the material contained in High Mysticism was only available as individual lessons and was brought together in book form for the first time. Although there were many errors in these first publications and many Bible verses were incorrectly quoted, I am happy to announce that WiseWoman Press is now publishing *High Mysticism* in the a corrected format. This corrected form was scanned faithfully from the original, individual lessons.

The next person to publish some of the Bible Lessons was Rev. Marge Flotron from the Ministry of Truth International in Chicago, Illinois. She published the Bible Lessons as well as many of Emma's other works. By her initiative, Emma's writings were brought to a larger audience when DeVorss & Company, a longtime publisher of Truth Teachings, took on the publication of her key works.

In addition, Dr. Carmelita Trowbridge, founding minister of The Sanctuary of Truth in Alhambra, California, inspired her assistant minister, Rev. Shirley Lawrence, to publish many of Emma's works, including the first three series of Bible Interpretations. Rev. Lawrence created mail order courses for many of these Series. She has graciously passed on any information she had, in order to assure that these works continue to inspire individuals and groups who are called to further study of the teachings of Mrs. Hopkins.

Finally, a very special acknowledgement goes to Rev Natalie Jean, who has worked diligently to retrieve several of Emma's lessons from the Library of Congress, as well as libraries in Chicago. Rev. Jean hand-typed many of the lessons she found on microfilm. Much of what she found is on her website, www.highwatch.net.

It is with a grateful heart that I am able to pass on these wonderful teachings. I have been studying dear Emma's works for fifteen years. I was introduced to her writings by my mentor and teacher, Rev. Marcia Sutton. I have been overjoyed with the results of delving deeply into these Truth Teachings.

In 2004, I wrote a Sacred Covenant entitled "Resurrecting Emma," and created a website, www.emmacurtishopkins.com. The result of creating this covenant and website has brought many of Emma's works into my hands and has deepened my faith in God. As a result of my love for these works, I was led to become a member of Wise-Woman Press and to publish these wonderful teachings. God is Good.

My understanding of Truth from these divinely inspired teachings keeps bringing great Joy, Freedom, and Peace to my life.

Dear reader; It is with an open heart that I offer these works to you, and I know they will touch you as they have touched me. Together we are living in the Truth that God is truly present, and living for and through each of us.

The greatest Truth Emma presented to us is "My Good is my God, Omnipresent, Omnipotent and Omniscient."

Rev. Michael Terranova
WiseWoman Press
Vancouver, Washington, 2010

LESSON I

Jacob's Prevailing Prayer

Genesis 32:9-12 Genesis 24:30

The subject of this lesson is "Prevailing Prayer." Jacob prevailed over conditions with his idea of what God ought to be and do. The "man" with whom he "wrestled all night till the morning," was his own idea of God. It is our privilege to see face to face our own idea of the Divine Being. It is our privilege to strengthen and empower that idea, with ability to prevail for us against our circumstances before we arrive among them.

If my idea of God is that he could — but will not — help me to be wise, free and at peace, I shall certainly handle that idea with every skill I can summon, to beg, drive or coax it to prevail against the follies that there is danger of my committing, against the limitations I am shutting myself into, against the pain I see ahead of me.

Nobody ever deals with any God higher than his own idea. A great many of us try to get our idea to work against the sun shining on the circus tent and horse race, but lo and behold, it rains on our prayer meeting, streaks the cathedral with lightning tracks, and leaves the circus and race course in happy weather. Then we roll up our eyes, clasp our vanquished fingers and murmur something about the "mysteries of Providence."

There is really no mystery about it. We were not good at empowering and nerving our idea of what the ruler of a world ought to be and do, which is all.

Here stands the "I" at the head of its mass of ideas. One of its ideas is its idea of God. Each "I" may infuse that idea with power enough to prevail over anything that confronts us. Jacob spent a whole night nerving and invigorating his idea of God with energy and skill to conquer Esau with. He felt that the task was a severe one. There is a saying that "a brother offended is harder to be won than a strong city." "Toward morning," he felt "a virtue going out" of his "I" into his "idea."

God Transcends Idea

Of course, if you and I do not take the trouble to run the virtue out of our "I" into our "idea," it is a poor, nerveless thing to meet "Esau" by any manner of means. It may be the spring and push of our personal mind and conduct, but God, the true God, transcends idea. He who has no idea of God, but knows that the "Great Fact" abides, will not feel that he must wrestle with "It" to make it smooth out his hard places for him. He will know it as the Entirely Unalterable, the Eternally Changeless. He will see that its works are eternal, unalterable, changeless, like itself.

He who has "Esau" to meet, viz., trials, may nerve any one of his ideas with his "I" substance and the next day have no trials at all. He will think God changed Esau's mind, and be grateful for the change — that is, he will think God's merciful kindness erased his trials. But no, it was only his skill in nerving his idea of God.

He was only practicing "Jacob." It was his battledore and shuttlecock of "suggestions." He played well. For all trials are formulated "suggestions." All victories over them are formulated "suggestions." God is not a "suggestion." He runs not in any race. He is against nobody and nothing. He is for nobody and nothing. He is the Impartial One. Jesus Christ preached this lesson in one text: *"Blessed are the poor in spirit for theirs is the kingdom."* (Matthew 5:3) He knew that their idea of God was that he is Spirit. The more they should empty themselves of their ideas, the more there would be left of them. Even the idea that God is Spirit gets set up finally as a fighting character, infused with ability to run against the trials well. Get free from it, or "pour," every poor, in it.

There is a doctrine of God very seldom enunciated, but called out by this chapter. We know first that the two ideas, "spirit and matter," are opposite terms. Our first lesson in metaphysics reads: "Matter is the unreal and temporal; Spirit is the real and eternal." Pantajali called these opposing ideas "pairs of opposites." The presentation of matter to spirit is the instant destruction of matter. If you wish to prove this, tell your brain that it is "spiritual, not material" a few times and see how clear and intelligent it will feel. Its weight will dissolve somewhat. Keep on with that talk to your brain, and it will become an entirely new instrument in the fingers of your language.

All To Become Spiritual

Now, then, this universe is to be seen as spiritual, entirely spiritual, by our whole race, so all our Bibles prophesy. But when it is seen as spirit, all spirit, and spirit is one of a "pair of opposites," how shall spirit know that it is spirit, since there is nothing to compare itself with? There is then at this point no spirit. Do you see this? Then you are "poor in spirit." It is a very free fact, is it not? It is "the handful of corn on the top of the mountain" of all the doctrines of the world.

Once Jesus preached that we must never "go down from the housetop" of our high and true knowledge of God "to take anything out of our house" full of ideas of God. He meant we were better off to keep our eye on the God who transcends our mass of ideas, and not try to work our ideas, Jacob like, to beat and push our way with.

While Jesus was in the garden and Mary was trying to touch him as a physical being, he told her she had not even yet turned her ideas to him as "spirit, not matter." So he said, *"Touch me not, for*

I have not yet ascended." (John 20:17) He gave the whole army of disciples a powerful treatment to turn their mind to the spirit entirely. This has always been called the "ascent of mind; the ascent of life."

The more spiritual your doctrine is, the more uplifted you will feel. If you wish to improve this, try reading over a few pages of the Bible, and then try reading some criticisms upon it. The book will cure your spine, relieve your pain, inspire you with courage. The criticism will pin your spine stiff, increase your pain, depress your heart.

One is the "ascent to the Father;" the other is the "prowl among tombs."

Jesus Christ said, "Woe unto them that are" swelled up with worldly schemes when this wonderful doctrine shall stream from on high like the lightning. They shall be so cumbered with their own former ideas they cannot run, they cannot fly. So now, *"Blessed are the poor in spirit,"* for they can ascend. They do not try to compel an idea to run ahead, like a battering ram, against poverty. They know there is no poverty. They do not try to believe that spirit is victorious over matter. They know that that is only another attempt of ideas to fight ideas. They do not attempt to put spirit against matter to dissolve matter. That which they call spirit, lo, it is but their idea still.

Ideas Opposed to Each Other

They have a houseful of ideas, but now that they are on the housetop of knowledge that ideas of good, ideas of spirit, are nothing but pairs of opposites engaged in combat, they do not use any of them. *"They rest from their labors and their works do follow them."* (Revelation 14:13) They know what that means: *"My spirit shall not strive."* (Genesis 6:3)

When the strife was over, Jacob saw God; not while the strife was on. If we have ceased from trying to make our ideas win among the battalions of ideas now ranging the fields of universal mind, we are ready to see that the morning of God hath dawned on our face.

That which transcends ideas — that is God. It is no wonder that the Brahmins taught restraint of thoughts, even to stopping them entirely, that truth might shine full on their faces. Our own Bible teaches, *"Be still and know that I am God."* (Psalms 46:10)

So I must understand that it was deep night with me while I was thinking I had hardships to meet which my idea of God would overcome if I would work it faithfully. It was past midnight on the way toward morning when I saw that there were no hardships, for free spirit had dissolved them. It is nearing dawn when I am willing to be poor in spirit. It is glad sunshine when I recognize the presence of One against whom there is no opposite pitted; even in name. That One is indeed now present.

There is no doubt about great "works following" all who recognize what is now here in its unalterableness. The unalterable must manifest itself everywhere. When the doctrines of opposites are ended, mind rests from its labors and its works do follow it. Jacob expressed it in Verse 30: *"I have seen God and my life is preserved."*

Inter-Ocean Newspaper, April 1, 1894

LESSON II

Discord In Jacob's Family

Genesis 37:1-11

The knowledge of truth is our Canaan. "Jacob dwelt in the land where his father was a stranger." Take the knowledge of that truth that sickness is unreality. When you know it, what transpires in your bodily condition? One little malady disappears, or a great one vanishes, according to whether you appreciate the truth much or little.

If you are one who appreciates that truth keenly, you will dwell in it. Some more statements of truth will be needed to feed your mind, to warm and nourish its other possibilities.

"I do not understand it," whine certain ones when told that disease is chimera, like the blindness of Charcot's subjects. By and by, they agree that it is so. They are dwelling within Canaan's borders. "I do not understand it," they whimper when told that poverty is as imaginary as disease. Directly, they discover that truth is not only *"God, thy health," (Jehovah-rapha - Jehovah makes whole)* (Exodus 15:26), but *"God, thy provider" (Jehovah-jireh - Signifies the I AM provider),* (Genesis 22:14). This pleases them and they are more firmly established in Canaan. They are Jacob preparing a Joseph with still further powerfulness.

For is the power of truth limited to saving you from shipwreck, healing you of rheumatism, clothing and feeding you? Nay, your knowledge of the stars that wheel in their orbits, of the shape of this planet, of the fourth dimension in space, will spring up like a seed long buried in a mummy case exposed to sunshine if you proclaim that matter is unreality, for the substance that will not permit anything but itself to exist is not matter.

It is wonderful how many unused powers lie ready to rise in bright splendor within you if you are bold enough to insist that there is only one mind, one substance, one power. Jacob set aside the law of punishment for sin by boldly ignoring sin in a fashion quite like the way the spiritual teachers of our time ignore disease.

Setting Aside Limitations

You may set aside limitation of any sort by boldly insisting that limitation is an unreal fence. *"I set before you an open door which no man can shut,"* said Jesus Christ. (Revelation 3:8)

If you are a patient or subject of Charcot, he tells you that your right foot is amputated. This causes you to limp. What sets you free? Knowledge that he is lying to you. If you are a subject or patient of the doctors of divinity, what idea has fenced off your powers and keeps you limping like one with his foot gone?

You know very well that these doctors are honestly convinced we are all *"conceived in sin and born in iniquity;"* (Psalms 51:5) *"Born to trouble as the sparks fly upward;"* (Job 5:7) *"Born to wax old like a garment;"* (Isaiah 50:9) "Born to die;" subject to disease; liable to err; some of us were born with little or no brains; some with much brains; some are cowards, some are thieves, some are brave and honest by inheritance, and some have their clutches on the necks of their fellow men. But I say unto you, these ideas are as false as Charcot's information that a potato is an apple, or a peach is an onion. I proclaim that the knowledge of what Jesus Christ is will set every one of these ideas aside and show us all alike wonderful in wisdom, strength and majesty.

Jesus Christ is that body of true principles which, when you once know them, will show you forth as a being not dependent upon brains for your understanding, and wholly independent of the favor of the human race for your opportunities. You will, by this set of principles, succeed in brilliancy of wisdom and entire absolution from old age, death and error.

If Jacob could "dwell in the land wherein his father Isaac was a stranger," (Verse 1) you also may dwell in a land of mind wherein your fathers were strangers.

"These are the generations of Jacob," (Verse 2) the prince of Israel. That is, whoever stands up and insists on truth independent of mortal suggestions, will see wonderful demonstrations. We "generate" manifestations by taking hold of our princehood. If I agree to one single proposition against my intelligence, I refuse my royalty of intelligence which was with me with God before the world was.

"Whom Shall I Believe?"

Jesus Christ says, *"I will give thee a mouth and wisdom which thine adversary shall not gainsay nor resist."* (Luke 21:15) But you tell me I cannot hold my own on this globe if the masters and the scholars set out to quench me. Whom shall I believe?

"I will destroy both the master and the scholar," said the Lord. (Malachi 2:12) Why? Because they "generate" on the side of "Bilhah and Zilpah." It is "Bilhah and Zilpah" who insist that man is dependent on brains for his intelligence and on opportunities of money or birth or personal excellences or agreement with reigning creeds for his getting on with mankind.

He needs nothing of the kind. He gets on most smoothly who takes truth just as it is. He who sees that intelligence fills the universe and brains are but statements of absence and presence thereof, declines the statement of absence and makes the statement of impartial presence. He takes his wisdom first hand. He faces all wisdom. "How hath this man letters, having never learned?"

He who sees that love fills the universe and that hearts are but statements of absence and presence theory, declines the statements of absence of love and makes the statement of impartial presence of love. He takes love at first hand. He faces all love. "How hath this man love, having never loved and never been loved?"

He who sees that goodness fills the universe and that convicts and tramps are but statements of absence thereof, declines the statement of absence of goodness; he may have been a tramp; he may have been a Joliet convict, but he then faces up the one impartial goodness. "How hath this man goodness, never having been good?"

Who are you shut up there in the reform school or tied to the typewriter? Do you not know that those things are but hypnotic stupors into which you are fenced by nodding your unconscious assent to the doctrines of men? Ho! Every one that thirsteth, to drink of the wells of his own love of freedom! Why do you take for your portion anything less than the free God? Have you not heard, have you not read, have you not known, that "I shall be satisfied when I awake?" And what shall wake up the seemingly stupid subjects of error?

On the Side of Truth

When the light that lighteth every man is proclaimed, there arise certain ones who "generate" or demonstrate on the side of truth. They are free from mistakes, free from poverty, free from disease, they understand their own worth in the universe. No man can shut down on their time. No man can shut down on their happiness. No man can shut down on their opportunities. Without friends they, by a new process, befriend the race. Without home, they shelter the world. Without possessions, they invest us all because they tell the truth. Truth shows us who we are, where we live, what we are doing. Truth sets us going on smooth pathways of life. Every other doctrine shall bow as Joseph's brothers' corn sheaves to the doctrine of the impartial omnipotent God in all men alike.

Every other doctrine shall bow, though once they were all in all to mankind as it is here proclaimed that even the sun and stars bowed down to Joseph, who in this lesson stands for young, newly spoken, advance truths about each man's own self.

"Joseph" means "he will add." So truth will indeed "add" new discovery after new discovery of your own wonderfulness. Now it is written that "Joseph's brethren envied him, but his father observed the saying." The astronomer thinks you must study stars for knowledge of stars, but Jesus Christ says, "Seek God and your knowledge of stars will transcend all that the brethren among star gazers declare." In old time language, they are "envious" at such an idea; in new time language, their stories are vanished myths like the diseases of those who have found out the truth about health.

Whoever watcheth his own inner light is Jacob, the Father. The reigning sectarian says Christ was buried and rose, but the "inner light" of truth as the Quakers who "observed the saying" shed its first beams on the doctrines of men, said Christ never was buried and Christ never rose. And the "inner light" of the Quakers was truth, which was the glory you had with the father before you became hypnotized by nodding assent to the winds of the sayings that you are of the world to get on with the world; that you must stay bound at the stake of your present lot till something transpires.

That "something" has transpired if you are ready, like Joseph in this 37th of Genesis, to tell boldly to "the sons of Bilhah and Zilpah," who are all the hypnotizers of our race, through schools, trades, religions, art, language, that you are not subject to them, though younger than they are (being, as it here says, only "seventeen years of age," which is the age at which truth keepeth her proclaimers forever and ever; herself being immortal youth), for you shall put their information under your feet, whether they fight well and long or yield now.

To know God is sure healing. To know God is sure support. To know God is sure protection. To know God is enough education, enough property, enough liberty.

Inter-Ocean Newspaper, April 8, 1894

LESSON III

Joseph Sold Into Egypt

Genesis 37:23-36

Strychnine, cocaine, arsenic are excellent tonics for people who have not learned the principle of inhaling vigor-producing mental ethers. Hate, enmity, curses are quickening tonics for minds that would easily lie back on tears of self-complacency.

Therefore, Jesus, the teacher, said much in praise of hate. *"Do good to them that hate you."* For this makes them hate your harder, and hate is the only medicine that will teach you how self-poised you can be. Every mind ought to be self-sustaining, self-inspiring. The mother hen, the mother cat, the mother eagle, understand this principle and practice it wisely.

Men and women practice this method of invigorating our intelligence without the conscious judgment of explaining why they are doing it.

They are as wonderfully led to hate us as the maternal fowl to rage against her offspring.

"Love your enemies." Why? Because they are producing chemical changes in the atmosphere round about your mind that will awaken it to knowledges you have no imagination of.

Get all the enemies you can by affirming omnipotent truth. "Blessed are ye" when, because of some mighty truth uttered by you years in advance of its acceptance by men, they "cast you into a pit," as the brethren did Joseph.

The fewer friends you have, the less effeminate your mind. It now leans on nothing. It is "woe to them that lean on the arm of flesh." Why? Because friends, money, adoring acquaintances are not something to lean upon, but something that hide the almighty arm of God.

So this lesson is a panorama of the history of one bold truth never swerved from when once uttered. Joseph means "he will add." Uttered truth is self-creative. Whatever you hear in the night watches, tell the world of it in the sunshine. Joseph saw and heard that he was a royal, a transcendent being, under whose feet the old creeds would fall. He told this aloud. The young truth glowed and transfigured and he never hung his head with regret of speaking it.

Yet he was not strong, nor brilliant because of it, till he was well hated. At the first dash of hate he stands utterly alone, fatherless, brotherless, friendless. Now he is for the first time alive with the spirit of what he has spoken. Now, for the first time, he realizes his own godhead. It is no wonder Jesus said, "Love your enemies," for their whispers are vitalizing, their shouts are inspiring. Chemically compounding them with our truth, we realize we are buoyed up and excited to utter grander truths.

Influence on the Mind

How good, how divine, is the alchemy of hate and cursing when the mouth has proclaimed a truth! If the mind were dull and negative before, it brightens and gleams with splendid fires now.

"He who hath led me to this way

Still on the way will show;

He who hath taught me of this way

Still more will make me know."

The Ishmaelites coming from Gilead, going down into Egypt, bought Joseph of his brothers.

"But yesterday and Caesar might have stood against the world,

Now none so poor to do him reverence."

But it was the unfriended Joseph whose greatness dignifies the pages of human history. It is Caesar's name that stands boldly forth on the tablets of unwritten names of those that failed him in his extremity. What is today's desolation but energy and brightness to that woman, that man, who knows one truth, and that one truth proclaimed has made his mind from that moment into another quality?

One does not need to keep his audible words continually going in order to generate hate. Thinking, realizing his inborn nobility, his rights in the universe, will breed it if one appreciates that it is because he came forth from heaven and brings God with him that he is a wonderful being.

The story of Joseph is the story of the "I AM" in any man when it is announced. Good works will not commend to courteous conduct. The brethren hated Joseph while he was serving them. It was not for being a good healer that they persecuted Jesus, but "because thou being a man makest thyself God."

Ishmael many years before Joseph's time, had been fed and strengthened in the wilderness by a miracle wrought through the chemistry of hate, and the note of payment came partially due to Abraham's descendant, Joseph, in the pit, and was entirely paid when Joseph fed his father and his brethren being utterly restored in honor.

Ishmael means, "Whom God hears." The God in Joseph caused his ears to hear the tramp of the traders' cattle and horsemen. No matter if we have to serve at trades and seem to be earning our bread like common slaves. Never mind if we have spoken of our inheritance from the all-owning God, and are still working at the counter or sewing machine. This is being Joseph. The day comes when we are the king's right hand.

Of Spiritual Origin

When we do not see any other way to do, only just as we are now doing for making our living, it is our ears hearing the Ishmaelites tramping. We hear the sounds of commerce, the ways of the trades, and are compelled to work in them. Let us know our mind. Is it a slave, or does it remember its origin? With the unquenchable truth that we are of spiritual origin, spiritual body, and spiritual power, we may work on till our miraculous genius breaks all bounds as Joseph's did when he stood before Pharaoh, King of Egypt, who exclaimed in awe: *"Can we find such a one as this is, a man in whom the spirit of God is?"* (Genesis 41:38) *"See, I have set thee over all the land of Egypt."* (Genesis 41:41)

This is all figurative. Egypt means "material things." Learning, art, science, manufactures: over all these the spiritually minded shall reign. The spiritually minded are now the meek of the earth, whose hour is striking to shortly take utter possession thereof.

Genesis and Revelation clasp hands on the sacred prophecy that in one hour shall the love of money, which now is "chief city," "queen of the world," be utterly prostrated and the kingdom of Zion be set up. Cannot every sovereign, every subject, be bought for gold? Therefore, his love of money is his queen, his king. His silent protest, his silent thought that with God no money consideration counts, is his meek idea, his Joseph, which as the people all get nearer and nearer one mind through international dealings, comes nearer and nearer to breaking out.

Do you not feel the great protest of the inner heart of mankind against putting us all to the service of money? Revelation promises freedom. Jesus promises freedom. Daniel promises freedom. Joseph prefigures freedom.

It is not gold itself, money itself, that is queen of the world, but love of money for what it has risen in our day to buy. Have you not read in the Book of Revelation how this love that has seduced men shall suddenly slip out of the mind of the race "in one hour," and the merchantmen, shipmen, buyers, and traders shall lament because buying and selling shall nevermore be upon the earth?

There is a way of living, which is not by the machinery of money, but by the divine proclamation of the silent protest now rapidly unifying itself. When this long-silent, meek "I AM that I AM" breaks forth, quickened by hate through ages, enlarged because uncherished through generations, empowering itself while said by all the world to be dead, mourned by the church as devoured, the heavens shall roll away as a scroll, the elements shall melt with fervent heat, "Zion awakes, redeemed without money" — Jesus is here. This is what the story of Joseph, hated by his brethren, sold into Egypt, mourned by Jacob, rising master of the world, means. The reading of this truth by you, agreeing with it even in the meekest region of your being, is clasping hands with the kingdom of God now.

Inter-Ocean Newspaper, April 15, 1894

LESSON IV

Object Lessons Presented In The Book Of Genesis

Genesis 41:38-48

Whoever wrote the Book of Genesis put great principles into object lessons. From this chapter, we learn that the man who breathes the atmosphere of the four accusations which "mortal mind" directs against him, and yet remembers that his real character is not anything less than God, after serving three years at breathing the fourth one, is acknowledged by all the world to be what he himself has been acknowledging.

It is the "natural," the "carnal," the "mortal" way to accuse mind, fourthly, of foolishness and ignorance, if it once proclaims and perseveres in believing that it came forth from "Spirit, not matter;" that its destiny is dominion over "the world, the flesh, and the devil."

The foolish and ignorant may neither speak in their own defense nor be regarded when speaking of or for their neighbors. Therefore, when you feel the breath of the fourth accusation blowing on your mind, keep silence. The beauty of Joseph was his three years' imprisonment in the white castle at Memphis, during which the inspiration of a commanding judgment was generated by his masterful silence.

The close confinement of yourself in the prison-house of your present circumstances, out of which you cannot seem to get, is on account of a supposed mistake you once made in conducting your affairs. While you are going through the straightenings caused by your supposed mistakes, do everything that comes in your way to do silently, patiently, communing with the God Presence only. The moment your mind gets all the information of uncomplaining silence, you will be set in authority over your circumstances.

Pharaoh, who represents material conditions, and men who judge by common sense, admits that it is only the Spirit of God in a man that can afford to be silent when appearances are all against him. *"God hath showed thee all this, there is none so discreet and wise as thou art."* (Verse 39)

Emerson says that great men are they who succeed in bringing other men around to their way of thinking after twenty years. What eternal principle have you believed in and guided your life by for fourteen years as Joseph, or twenty years as Emerson did?

That is not an eternal principle, which says, "I would like to be honest. I started out to be honest, but I found I must meet men on their own ground and beat them with their own weapons." This principle of action must end in sudden disappearance of your health, reputation, happiness. It has no inspiring life in it.

The principle that has unkillable life in it must be a Jesus Christ one. The author of Genesis proposes that we regard ourselves as Spirit, and look upon all things as good. If we so persist, we shall find ourselves to be onlookers at a set of picture plays figuring out our status on our own principles. Jesus of Nazareth took the principles of himself and God as identical, and all that was real were his words. Nothing else amounted to anything at all. "Profiteth nothing," he said.

Joseph took the principle that he had no need to be agreeing with church or state or school dicta. He was transcendent being, needing not that any man should teach him books that he might know books, needing not to earn money or inherit it to be rich, needing not to practice a system of great thoughts to have a masterful mind. He took the simple stand of his own God-being. He stood there fourteen years and all Egypt shouted: *"Abreck! Abreck!" which means "Rejoice! Rejoice!" or as here translated, "We bow the knee."* (Verse 43)

Three years of that time he was in a tight place. In Psalms 105:17-18, we read that the fetters on his feet hurt him sorely, but he did not complain. Part of that time he was in a pit. Ten years he was a slave of Potiphar, captain of the guard of Pharaoh. All because he discovered that he was not flesh, but spirit; not carnal nature, but God nature from first to last; and never yielded his point!

This is the only greatness, then, a principle secretly maintained. It attends to its people when it gets ready. And it never fails to attend to its people at the right moment exactly.

"And Pharaoh called Joseph's name Zaphenath-paneah; and he gave him to wife Asenath, the daughter of Potiphera, priest of On."

"Zaphenath-paneah" means "Governor of the living One." Twice seven years the boy had served the high statement, "I am governor over material things by my spiritual prerogatives," as his father, Jacob, had served twice seven years for Rachel. "Fourteen" is a mystic number consecrated to patience. One cure in metaphysics represents our "patience" quality. It is the cure of our state of subordination to the dictum of associates. A bodily cure accompanies it. The moment we get away from the chain of silent endurance, we are new creatures. A new set of circumstances arises. A new bodily vigor seizes us.

At this point, Jesus made a whip and whipped the traders like a master in a southern cotton field. It was a wise chastising. Only one who had been set free from patience by serving patience could possibly strike me wisely with a whip of cords. Only one who came forth from God and understood the cure of leprosy, the raising of Lazarus instantaneously, could afford to call me a "scribe, Pharisee, hypocrite." An imitator of the "Master of Denunciation" makes bungling work of it. He has some sickness strike him to make him as an imitator. He has to turn and twist financially. The "Master of Denunciation" is governor of finances in the sight of all men. He is a handsome exhibition of the brilliant smiles of health through and through. Not till you understand raising the dead and turning poverty and hunger into plenty are you ready to chastise, call names, run down your fellow man scientifically.

The Old Testament lessons are exceedingly practical. They corroborate by actual histories the principles announced by Jesus Christ. We may take them on the extremely material plane and be benefited by studying them. We may take them on the mental or intellectual plane, or by ideas, and we see how to run our minds with more skillfulness. We may take them on the plane of regarding ideas of mind and physical movements as both equally chimerical and symbolic, and stand aside from the universe free as the Changeless One.

On the plane of ideas, we are told by this Bible section, that a mystic beauty steals over the face and form after a high statement has been held its rightful length of time. It is told by "giving Joseph Asenath" the favor of Isis. When Isis is unveiled for the whole world's vision, the world's beauty is eternal. Nothing fades and grows unsightly.

Beautiful presence of the spirit in our midst is Isis, the Holy Spirit of God. Any eternal truth secretly maintained will cause it to beautify our faces with the light of its presence visibly. Did not Jesus Christ say that whoever would make his name their breath as the priests of On inhaled and exhaled Isis-Osiris, and as Brahmins inspired and expired Om, would have the Holy Spirit? What is so wonderful as the Holy Spirit? Its fine fire radiance is the mystic breath which understanding of our own spirit gives. Whosoever has the Holy Spirit through Christian science lessons is master of the corn and the gold of all earth. Whosoever gives up his high statements before he has given them the Joseph service has no more masterfulness over the poverty, the hunger, the unequal distribution, the debts, the panics of this age than he had before he used them.

"By their fruits ye shall know them." (Matthew 7:20) The hour pushes close. Many a voice urges us to let go of the truths which Jesus said keep. This lesson of Joseph comes floating over the centuries from the land of the Sphinx and the pyramids, from the city of On, where priestly love of art never equaled the splendor hinted at of what the Holy Presence would work for mankind when Jesus should be born with a name within whose folded sounds is bread for the world without money and without price.

Did you ever believe that it was folly to make a spiritual affirmation high out of the reach of your personal experience, but hold it through fair and foul, dark and light, friendship and enmity, till it should take you on its own wings whither it would?

If not, then you have not seen what the story of Joseph signifies. You have put aside the authority of Jesus, "keep my sayings"; you are easily tempted. You are of them that the prophets promised who should say in these days, "What profit?" and "Where is the Lord?" The cure you want to see accomplished is the one which patience only, and that on your own part, will work out. Nobody will work the cure for you, which stands for your own proposition, steadfastly, silently maintained. Nobody can breathe for you. The patience may not be required for fourteen years as we reckon time, but it certainly is past the span where you are seemingly in need of a friend, and those who seem wisest dispute the wisdom of your course past and present, because you seem to be in the prison of misfortune. Joseph judged not by appearance. Though he stood alone, he was not alone. The Lord, of whom he had been speaking, to whom, as within himself he had been speaking, suddenly appeared as a master.

"Who could abide the day of his coming?" (Malachi 3:2) Could famine stay in Joseph's sight? Could friendlessness be a state of his life? Could

those whom he knew, friend and foe, be poverty stricken?

In this hour the "famine of the land" can be outwitted only by high statements concerning your own divinity, from which you do not swerve till their light breaks over your life and your omnipotent spirit takes possession.

Inter-Ocean Newspaper, April 22, 1894

LESSON V

"With Thee Is Fullness Of Joy"

Genesis 45:1-15

There is a mental chemistry and there is a material chemistry. A "chemical" is that "resulting from the operation of the forces upon which composition and decomposition depend, as chemical changes, chemical combinations." (Webster's definition)

In material combinations of substance we find two ingredients uniting and making what might be called annihilation. Camphor gum and alcohol unite and no extra space is required. Ether and the alcohol then unite with air, and there is nothing visible left. Lo! Anger of mind and repentance unite, and only the repentance is left. Repentance of mind exposed to the sunshine of forgiveness, and what is left? What so ethereal as pure joy? This, at its supreme is God, the sun and breath of the universe.

On this plan of explaining Brahman, the Oriental philosopher declares that all substance in the universe can unite chemically and occupy only a mathematical point, and that all the states of mind now filling the universe may chemically unite and make the God Mind, which is the "inconceivably small one," the "one point."

Instead, then, of teaching us to "watch for God omnipresently external, the mystic Easterner tells us to focus our mind to an inconceivably fine point, till all our angers, criticisms, griefs, loves, hates are — by the chemistry of mind — resolved into the one unnamable center.

The attention of thousands upon thousands of intelligent and noble men and women is being called to this manner of resolving all things into divinity. If I would be entirely fair in my interpretations of these Bible lessons, I must turn over the leaves of every genuine book of spiritual teachings that I can lay my hands on and report those explanations which have been accepted by the wise and sincere of all ages as practicable.

India Favors Philosophic Thought

Max Muller, in *What Can India Teach Us?* says: "If I were asked under what sky the human mind has most fully developed some of its choicest gifts, has most deeply pondered on the greatest problems of life, and has found solutions of some of them which will deserve the attention even of those who have studied Plato and Kant, I should point to India."

Today's Bible lesson teaches the chemistry of repentance and forgiveness. It brings forth joyousness. With these chemical writings, prosperity is manifest. Thus on the mental plane, a state of mind is promised to compel material operations. Joy has a charm about it to attract good luck.

Grief has a charm about it to attract misfortune. Socrates taught this. The Bible teaches it.

Sometimes the Bible shows that we run into the consequences of our former states of mind. The envy of Joseph's brethren ran into Joseph of Heliopolis.

What a demonstration took place; the eastern philosopher would see the clash of the good and the evil state of mind. The materialist would see only that Joseph outwitted his brethren.

Sometimes, the one point of Being, which is divinity, is called a lightning spark. It is said to be the center of every man's being. When a man's mind thinks like the God at his center, he demonstrates healing power like Jesus; he demonstrates prosperity for his neighbors like Joseph.

Sometimes, these laws of thoughts are explained by metaphysicians by geometrical symbols, as angles and circles and points. Pythagoras said that "God geometries." For instance, as a horizontal line meets a perpendicular and makes a right angle, so a right purpose in the heart touches the everlasting purpose of God and a noble character appears in the world's life.

What These Figures Impart

This is neither foolish nor wicked language of explanation where a noble purpose, a high evangel is intended by these figures of speech: "Who are these that lie in wait for the righteous to condemn them for a word?"

"And Joseph said unto his brethren: Be not grieved or angry with yourselves that ye sold me hither, for God did send me before you to preserve life." (Verse 5) Here is the denial of sin. "God is too pure to behold iniquity." He who is most like God sees less sin. When his mind comes in contact with sin, it annihilates it. Only one mind is left. This can be applied to the gambler, the embezzler, the fratricide. There is an association of mind, which results in one mind. Joseph had got his mind so potent after twenty-two years of training that he was able to make wickedness dissolve in his presence like camphor gum in alcohol.

In metaphysical healing, you will find that you cannot cure a case of dropsy if you hate the sensuality of the man who lugs the dropsy. Neither can you cure him of sensuality while it is so real to you. The mind of you is not trained like Joseph's. You must go on somewhat longer thinking of the divine spark in all men, till a moment arrives when the divine in man is all that you see in all men. Then the dropsy man with his veil of sensuality will not be visible. His God nature will be plain in your sight. This will cure him.

Suppose it takes you twenty-two years of concentrated attention to the divine in man to realize it? Joseph took twenty-two years to train his mind to dissolve the iniquity of his brothers. In his sight, they were no longer wicked.

Now, while we hang and imprison our fellowmen for crimes, we see that we have no heads of state who have spent twenty-two years thinking so constantly of the divinity in all men that when the crimes appear in their presence a chemical change transpires, leaving only the divine.

The Errors of Governments

Heads of state try to imitate the chemistry of godliness by hangings, guillotines, electricity, imprisonment for life, etc. This seems to leave their minds alive and alone on the boards of human action. The criminals are annihilated. Age after age of this kind of chemistry has been going on. Has it lessened embezzlers, seducers, gamblers?

The imitation of truth and methods of annihilation must remain forever unsuccessful. Only the true is successful. Joseph is able to say, *"So now, it was not you, but God."* (Verse 8) Our heads of state must be able to say this.

About once in so long, a great famine seizes upon every nation. In our country it is always a money famine. It is always visible when the greedy mind of the nation faces up some new religious idea that is gaining ground.

Once it was the idea that there are no black or white in Christ Jesus. Then it was that all have an equal right to health. This day's famine comes from the religious proclamation that all men are equally divine with Jesus Christ. The proposition started out over the mental atmospheres when greed was great.

Thus did Joseph's great proposition, "I am God," start out when the greed of Israel's people waxed great. After twenty-two years, they collided. Joseph's proposition had unkillable substance in it. The brethren's greed of gain, greed of fame, greed of power, disappeared. Hath not a whole world waxed greatly greedy altogether today? Hath the idea that "God in man is his only substance" ability to annihilate greed in a whole world? I am sure that it has. All Bibles prophecy that there shall be finally one kingdom only left on earth.

From India, with her One Point, whose name is Brahman; from Arabia, with her One Presence, whose name is Allah; from Egypt, with her Father-Mother Nourisher of all, whose name is Osiris-Isis; from Persia with her Shining Light whose name is Ormuzed (or Oromasdes, the Grecianized form of the Zoroastrian deity, Ahura-Mazda); from Palestine, with her everlasting Word, which is God; we get the same scientific calculation: in that day shall the God of harmony set up a kingdom which shall consume all other kingdoms.

There is no harmony like the knowledge that not only is the preacher who speaks what the church papers approve divine from center to circumference, but Prendergast also is divine in all extent.

If it takes twenty-two years of attention to this One Point, to be able to dissolve or annihilate iniquity, I shall then and there only be Joseph, capable head of state.

Inter-Ocean Newspaper, April 29, 1894

LESSON VI

Change Of Heart

Genesis 50:14-26

Joseph had practiced one state of mind twenty-two years. Whenever he came into the immediate presence of other people of an opposite state of mind to his own, a chemical change occurred.

Eleven criminals (his brethren) stood in a row before him while he was governor of Egypt, and such was the mental suffering of them that while the chemistry of resolving their mind state into his was transpiring, they wept aloud and cried, *"Forgive us our trespass."* (Verse 17)

"And Joseph wept when they spoke unto him." (Verse 17)

One point of last Sunday's lesson is reviewed in Verse 17 of this one, viz., no man is fitted to be a governor of state until his mind has been trained to chemicalize the criminal classes so that by contact with him, they repent in honest humiliation as before God.

Whoever as a criminal is thus prostrated, has one everlasting truth for his consolation: "Their sins will I remember no more against them."

All religious teachings have this one intention of making nothing of sinfulness by a state of mind. They do not urge jails, reformation, poor houses; no, but change of heart. And the change of heart they urge over and over is produced by two processes:

a) First, by taking an aphorism (a concisely stated truth) opposite to the experience and holding it as a persistent thought till the mind is set to it as an instrument is set to a key-note, as Joseph did.

b) Second, by coming into direct contact with such a mind as every head of state is supposed to have (according to religion), "and suffering the swift change of heart which had been likened to the fermentation of acid and alkali mingling in a chemist's jar, as Joseph's eleven brothers did; as the thief on the cross did.

When an aphorism has wrought its mission, you will discover that to you there is no sin in the heart of your fellowman. Then if you say this aloud to those who do not accept or have not practiced whispering your aphorism, they immediately accuse you of licensing iniquity.

Religion As A Science

It is high time that religion were taught as a science. The error in a preacher's reasoning is discoverable quickly if you know the twelve points of science taught in all Bibles alike.

Which is better, to hang a man or change his heart? How do you change his heart? By being in the opposite state of heart yourself. If you are in a state of heart where his crime is crime to you, what is the difference between your point of view and his?

Just in matter of like and dislike. That is all. He likes it. You do not. The crime is as real a transaction to your sight as his.

But religion teaches that the right view is not to judge after the sight of the eyes nor after the hearing of the ears. The God state of mind is to see God and nothing else than God every where, every instant.

"He beholdeth not iniquity," Joseph finally arrived at this state. Jesus was there all the time. If this religion irritates you, it is a sign that you are experiencing a chemical change. If you call it a sophistry (deceptive reasoning) or license to sin, you are being secretly undermined in your present religious views. Soon you will believe this very word. You cannot help it any more than the eleven criminals arrayed before Joseph could help repenting.

Notice in this lesson that Joseph promises to nourish the eleven criminals and their little ones (Verse 21) because they were meek, which having done for over fifty years he chose to dwell in another realm where he could work out the proposition, "there is no death." He had finished the work belonging to his one idea, "I am supreme."

There is no record of any having yet taken the proposition, "There is no death," and turning their minds so to it that they are now visibly among us, being, as reckoned by years, over 100 or so. Some, however, left no material remains when they departed, as Moses, Elijah, Enoch. On this subject, Joseph was silent indeed. He agreed with the rest of the world and at the age of 110 (Verse 26) he said, *"I die ... and ye shall carry up my bones from hence."* (Verses 24-25)

On this subject, Jesus said much and is now often visible to mankind, intending to be shortly visible to all men alike, His mystic treatments having fulfilled their purpose.

The Number Fourteen

This lesson repeats the name Joseph fourteen times. When a Bible chapter repeats a name many times, its intention is to give us a metaphysical treatment on the line, which the name signifies.

Fourteen is a number consecrated to double fulfillment. Your own mind is set to a six day's task and then rest on its seventh day. The appearance of your world is changed by six day's performances, and on the seventh satisfies you with changeless perfection.

Each aphorism held in mind has six actives and one still. It moves on nature's face to make things demonstrate to prove itself. All the aphorisms of religious science are twelve. They all make the same round of change. He who can concentrate the meaning of the whole twelve statements of religious science into one is able to accomplish wonders quickly. Peter converted 3,000 by one lesson. He was already convinced himself and compelled conviction easily.

When certain Orientals wish you to receive the mental treatment of a word, they tell you to draw in your breath and repeat the word, hold the breath repeating the word; exhale the breath repeating the word.

This lesson from the Orient has the same secret purpose when it repeats the word, which means that your forgiving spirit shall increase, and increase while your attention is fixed upon it in the form of a story. The book of Genesis is an old-fashioned novel with a "motif."

Paracelsus said that reading the book of Revelation over and over would stimulate and draw forth your hidden magical powers.

By magical powers, he meant those unused faculties of man whereby he can heal by thought at a distance, stop crimes by his eyes, illuminate a room by a turn of his hand, as the adept did for Hensoldt, the German traveller, and many other performances without material aid.

So the story of Joseph stimulates the forgiving spirit and enlarges and increases your influence for good. It is quite a chemical change to the unforgiving chord in your mind. It is a chemical change to your inferiority among your fellowmen. It is impossible to read the story of Joseph from beginning to end without finding yourself more or less enlarged in the estimation of your fellow-beings.

Thus the story of Joseph has for part of its "motif," your high place in the estimation of mankind.

A certain youth who had never read the Bible till he was eighteen years of age exclaimed:

"Why, it is a book of magic! Look here, now, you read over and over an obscure passage and suddenly you are wide awake with a new piece of information, which the passage has not alluded to. You are told to watch a white or blue lily of the field and a new way of making your living will be shown you. The ant is a microscope to convey wisdom, though ostensibly to set you hustling. The lightning watched shall cause your thoughts to demonstrate instantly. Even the sentence, *'as the lightning shineth from the east unto the west,'* (Matthew 22:27) has the effect of a metaphysical change to make you do something promptly."

Divine Magicians

Moses, Elisha, Daniel, Jesus, were magicians of a divine sort of whom the mighty Chaldean sorts were spurious imitators. There do indeed seem to be legitimate processes of bringing things to pass by a set to of the mind. I do not wonder that the metaphysicians have said, "Mind is God." Mind "will bring out just as much if drawn upon by Coxey and his crew, as if drawn upon and marched out by Napoleon. It is not the outward appearance that treats the race, but the "motif."

Another who investigated all the Bibles said they were all works on the magic of the divine mysteries. One man without eyeballs had his attention so transfixed by certain parts of the Christian Scripture that the eyeballs began to grow and the sight thereof to generate. Many have received to the magic of the name Jesus Christ ofttimes repeated. All the majesty of Joseph, the sinewy endurance of Jewry, the prosperity of Abraham, the splendid diction of David, the knowledge of Solomon, are focused into it. *"In My Name shall the Gentiles trust."* (Matthew 12:21)

It changes the constitution and quality of each thought as it conies face to face -with it by repeating it silently. With its mysterious chemistry it transmutes poor, inferior, incompetent minds into noble beings, able to rise by the cross of ignominy into the adoration of a globe as in chariots of shiny gold across morning highways of fairer lands than sun ere shone on. *"The meek shall inherit the earth."* (Matthew 5:5) None so meek as they who read the Scriptures over and over without attempting either to put their own construction upon them or trying to reconcile erudition with their seeming discrepancies. Who so meek as he that lets them do with him what they will? "Teach," said Jesus.

The inheritance of sons of kings is yours; the greatness of kings at their untold best is yours; the ascension on happy wings of light out of your present sorrow is yours who read in meekness.

Inter-Ocean Newspaper, May 6, 1894

LESSON VII

Israel in Egypt

Exodus 1:1-14

One of the greatest of mystic secrets is that of multiplying and replenishing substances by a state of mind. Elisha did it nine hundred years before Jesus of Nazareth, when he multiplied twenty loaves to enough to feed one hundred hungry young men at the theological seminary of Gilgal.

The first commandment given to spiritual man incumbered by notions of obligation to obey matter was to keep his understanding of handling all things according to his own choice. "Multiply, replenish, subdue, the earth." The instant man thought the earth could dictate to him a drowning principle in water, a poisoning quality in poppy heads, a regulation of sowing, reaping, baking, for barley and wheat-bread, man was under subjection, he was not master.

Elisha and Jesus stepped out of the psychologic chains of other men's agreement with the dictating rise of matter. They obeyed God only, and subdued water to its proper state of solidity, or to its fluidity when that was most convenient to themselves without waiting for winter time to freeze it or summer to thaw it.

Wheat became plastic when they touched it with their fingers. It never asked for a bed of warm loam to repose in or for a husking and grinding experience before being fit to eat. It dared not presume so far.

Whether these peerless manufacturers loved the substances that obeyed them or declared them pure unrealities, as we have had explained by pietists and metaphysicians, this lesson does not consider; what it calls attention to its one fact, that is, he who subdues fire is not he who is obliged to circumvent it by beating it out on the grass plot where he wants to walk, but he who can forbid it to burn him. It is not written of you that if you know God it shall be so? "When thou walkest through the fires thou shalt not be burned, neither shall the flames kindle upon thee."

Principle of Opposites

The Bible lessons have called attention to a manufacturing principle of opposites, both in states of mind and in material things. Acid and Alkali commingling manufacture a new base. Recognition of the spirit in man, or what Joseph called the God in man, commingling with the man's consciousness of guilt manufactures meekness. Meekness is invariably followed by prosperity. "The meek shall inherit the earth." "I will nourish you and your little ones."

Majesty meeting inferiority manufactures the efficient Jesus Christ. "The Son can do nothing only what he seeth the Father do." "Honor and fortune exists to him who always recognizes the neighborhood of the great, always feels himself in the presence of high causes."

When I feel incompetent if I remember who is nigh me with an opposite feeling I shall not fail.

"Behold I am against thee, saith the Lord." The recognition of a noble power pitted against me, utterly and absolutely opposed to me, enables me, enlarges me. *"There arose up a new king over Egypt, which knew not Joseph."* (Exodus 1: 1-14) And his not knowing the adding principle caused the people he did not like to increase greatly. Joseph stands always for the multiplying and replenishing principal in all things.

Power of Sentiment

We as a race are governed by king public sentiment who knows nothing whatsoever of the actual principle of addition and therefore when public sentiment institutes a temperance movement he adds more and more beer barrels to those he had on hand before his movement. When he institutes an army to fight negro slavery, he multiplies slavery by white slavery. Is it not the bitter cry of our time that most of men are slaves to their neighbors? Is it not another cry that intemperance is increasing?

Now if king public idea can understand Joseph, or the adding principle, he can multiply and replenish free and undisturbed citizens throughout all the lands, instead of slaves and rum.

Whoever takes account of the Almighty on the subject of fire, bread, money, opium, will perform the office of king over these things. He is the Almighty to them.

Man generally recognizes the opposition of one loaf to multiplying itself to ten loaves independent of planting wheat. Therefore the loaf performs the office of king over him and makes him labor on a farm at $1 a month in Russia or $1 a day in America.

But Jesus Christ saith: *"Labor not for the meat that perisheth."* He calls attention to the fowls of the air which "sow not, neither do they reap, nor gather into barns." He speaks of no labor except the transforming of mind by planting itself directly face to face with the great opposition mind, which no man can recognize without giving up his mind. "No man can see my face and live." He must become me. If he has imagined he must obey matter I make him master over matter. If, he is humiliated by the bread and meat and money of his world all traveling into the hands of a certain few, I in him command the bread and meat and money to travel into equal distribution among all men.

Opposition Must Enlarge

"Behold, I am against thee, saith the Lord." Recognize my opposition. Be lost in it and subdue the earth."

Whoever looking to man sees opposition that which opposes must enlarge. Whoever looking toward material things sees their opposition to his wishes must see them enlarge as opposite. He who sees his money opposing his wish to multiply will see his money become totally *non est*. Poverty is an enlarged opposite.

The opposition which is recognized must own the situation. Therefore, Jesus recognizing the opposing God — not the opposing water — was master of water.

Recognizing the opposing God — not the opposing Lazarus — he was master of Lazarus. The opposition he recognized was on the subject of work. He had been trained as a boy to plant and reap, but God is against that order of things, and he recognized it. He had been trained as a boy to bury his friends, but God is against that order, and he recognized it. Therefore he gave thanks aloud.

The King of Egypt saw opposition in the sons of Jacob, where there was none, and multiplied them greatly. The sons of Jacob saw opposition in the bricks and straw, where there was none and it is here recorded that "Egyptians made their lives bitter with hard bondage in mortar, and in brick, and in all manner of service in the field; all their service wherewith they made them serve, was with rigor." The opposition that we recognize governs us. God is most certainly against all the practices of our present civilization. He is against our system of manufacturing food, clothes, machines, scholars, preachers, musicians, and artists. We have supposed he favored them, but Jesus teaches differently. The sooner we recognize his opposition the sooner the Jesus Christ system of manufacturing scholars and bread will flourish in our midst.

Inter-Ocean Newspaper, May 13, 1894

LESSON VIII

The Childhood of Moses

Exodus 2:1-10

"Egypt was then really glorious, Rome had not been thought of. Greece was a den of robbers. There was not a refined people in all Asia. At that time there was but one radiant spot on the globe, and that was Egypt, where were found the acme of the world in all philosophy, in all art, in all religion."

And in the prime of her splendor Egypt despises and dreads her Hebrew slaves, because they multiply and replenish. When Egypt laid her hand of oppression on her slaves "they prayed unto their God." The heavier the hand the more ardent their prayers, till one mighty day nature gathered together her forces and put a young child into their midst, with a fire in his eye caught from the altars that kindle irresistible greatness.

"What the spirit promises nature will perform."

When a world shall pray all men shall be kindled as gods. "I said ye are gods." When a nation prays one heart is kindled by greatness. When a woman prays one event is kindled with prosperous beauty. When a church prays a new pastor ascends her pulpit steps with a new order of eloquence.

Something oppresses sorely and a people, a world, a man prays wisely. It takes the great oppression and the wise prayer to forge the great answer. This principle works likewise with individuals as with nations. Your rebukes and rebuffs which you are visiting upon that one, may hurt him to the death, but he knows how to pray. Rebuke and rebuff, sit in judgment and override him every chance and every day, but he knows how to pray.

He is at a disadvantage on every hand; no eye pities and nor arm brings salvation, but he still prays. You are shocking the forces of air and sea, sky and dust together to kindle a new light in his eye, a new fire in his tongue, a new action in his life.

How New Fires Are Enkindled

That new splendor is Moses. That which you have struck as steel against flint shall kindle a flame that will burn you up and out, as Egypt in her pride, but one who has prayed, while you have rebuked and pushed to the wall, shall arise and shine, for the lightning of God is kindled by your opposition. So did papal oppression strike against the prayers of a people and kindle a Luther; so did human ownership strike fires with the prayers of black mothers in Southern cabins and kindle a Lincoln. So shall the owners of the gold of our country refusing to use for the people strike fire in this hour against the prayers of the multitudes of poverty-stricken, unpitied masses, and kindle an irresistible Moses in finance. There's a young thing growing up in our midst this day, at the sound of whose voice the money-holder shall tremble as the Ramses of Egypt at the sound of the voice of young Moses. Each age, each nation, each church, each individual may know that when its hour is blackest its redemption draweth nigh. Each country, as each heart, knoweth its own bitterness. The 2,000,000 Israelite's knew why their hard work and willing offices were not rewarded. The only power on the globe was then Egypt. She had all the advantage and meant to keep it.

The masses today know why they are not paid for hard work and willing service. There is but one power on the globe this day; it is the Egypt of our time. You know what it is. It is the money power. Face it up and describe its nature and possibilities. Explain how much the tyrant can do when a people know how to pray. When you tell the truth about the nature and possibilities of money the truth will be as mighty as Moses to "let my people go."

The Childhood of Moses

Truth Is Restless

Whenever a truth is born there have been oppression and prayer meeting in collision as a dark cloud meets a charged atmosphere. Truth is as restless as lightning. What is the truth about the dark cloud that hangs over our people? What was the truth about the dark hand held over the Israelites when Moses was born of the house of Levi? Its power is only as strong as the hand of Ramses. Its time is closing. How shall its fall be demonstrated? That is a secret with God. "I will lead thee by a way that thou hast not known." Who shall arise to personify deliverance? The mighty one cometh.

When a heart feels profound sadness at its situations and prays, its answer is sure, but the way of its answer is no more known than the path of the lightning. Neither is the time of its answer. "The times and the seasons no man knoweth." But "can ye not discern the signs if the times?" When the gloom is deep, even to anguish, a young thing is growing in its ark.

Pharaoh had ordered all the male children of the Hebrews slain. But the one only male child who had any fire of danger in him for Pharaoh he left alive and nourished at his own table. The unkillable, undefeatable thing is the answer to prayer. Something tiny as the "hidden man of the heart" of whom the Hindoos speak as "greatest of the great," of whom Peter speaks as the incorruptible one, is growing up among us. It is a new knowledge of the principle of human equality because of the spiritual equality of all men. Are the black slave's prayers as potential as Beecher's? Is the fire at the God point of Douglas identical with the fire at the heart of Jesus? Is there any black or white, scholar or ignoramus, at the starting point of man?

Man Started from God

There at their starting point our new religion watches all men at this hour. The proud and the wise agree about that starting point, and when speaking of it admit that though the only spark of man's first estate is now left to him yet indeed he started from God. Cannot you see that this admission is dangerous to class distinctions and caste differences, dominion and subjection master and scholar, employer and servant? Cannot you see the watched point enlarging in some mysterious fashion and shining as a coming unquenchable glory of fire to burn up the chaff of false estimates of men among men?

What have many Egyptians of our day declared but that the new religious propositions are dangerous? Do they not feel that it is high time to rouse and suppress them? Yet right at their tables, in their halls of learning, even in their pulpits and editorials they are nourishing the only one of all the new religious propositions that has storage of menace in it and that is the one they glory in admitting, namely, that at his starting point man is God.

Have you ever read of that principle whereby an absent, invisible object watched by the concentrated attention of mind, will finally come plainly into sight with all its accompaniments? Do you know of any people whose whole mind is now concentrated toward the divine starting point, the God origin in all men alike?

That is the little one who is to come "terrible as an army with banners." Some think that because the pitiful hordes that now tramp over our land are covered with the "slime and pitch" ignorance and inefficiency, as poor little weeping Moses was hidden by his mother, that it is not the wail of the deathless deliverer whom the high and mighty are to nourish as their most honored principle. But it is. It is the very first cry of the baby *"among the flags by the rivers brink."* (Exodus 2:1-10.) They who watch for the coming of the mighty spirit as night watchers for the morning recognize the one principle whether marching in the weeping hordes or smiling at the banquet boards of the mighty. Their prayers are being answered. "A little one shall become a mighty army, and a small one a strong nation." If the magnates of our age want, like Ramses II, of old, to strangle the one little Moses that menaces their money, their class distinctions, caste privileges, servant and master principles, they must throttle that baby idea that is now being nourished by their own learning, namely, that at the starting point man is God.

Inter-Ocean Newspaper May 20, 1894

LESSON IX

Moses Sent As A Deliverer

Exodus 3:10-20

At one of the fetes given to Napoleon in Paris the words of this day's scripture lesson were placed over his throne in letters of gold *"I am that I am"*. (Exodus 3)

The golden text is like unto it: *"Fear thou not, for I am with thee."* The "I am that I am" is self-existent unchangeable living God, whose everlasting abode is in every man and every object alike without respect of place or person. That which is self-existing is an indestructible element. It is the everlasting substance. It runs like a tideless river through us all alike. The so-called "great of the world" have been those who consciously or unconsciously leaned upon it as an inward power that moved and girded them.

The unconscious looking toward it from generation to generation breeds kingship. There is not a crowned head or crown prince of Europe in whose eye there is not left a fire flame of that gaze of his ancestor's mind on the primordial principle within him.

As all those crowned heads are now turning themselves away from it, the mutterings of dissatisfied subjects are heard on the night winds of time. With their turning aside the dominion of man over man shall cease, for the truth of the kingly inheritance of all men now speeds the fine lines of a new dawn on our race.

What Science Proves

Science proves that the priests and the prophets were right when telling what a being called God is and can do. But science explains what that being is and what understanding of that being can accomplish.

Science shows that the "I Am that I Am" of the prophets of antiquity is the primordial substance, the self-existing river of life, wisdom, and power, flowing through all things alike.

Science shows that even an unconscious recognition of this principle will make a man self-confident, self-persisting, and self-prospering.

Frederick the Great and Napoleon both leaned upon this reliable substance within themselves, but Napoleon began to look away from it at about 40 years of age. By thus turning aside his unconscious mind he showed his plebeian ancestry.

Frederick was not afraid of the babble. "Put the placard lower, where all the people can read it," he said to those who were nailing some printed condemnations of himself on the public walls.

But Napoleon kept spies out to protect his name from reproach. So far-reaching and keen-eyed was his espionage of everywhere that Mme de Stael wrote: "Europe has become a great net, which entangles you at every turn."

Who are you that fear when the eternal God is your refuge and underneath are the everlasting arms? It is plebeian to doubt your competency. It is King of Kings and Lord of Lords to know your foundations to "keep your eye in them", to understand how to rely upon them single-handed and alone. Understanding the principle of undefeatable, being through the science brought out by the six years' Bible course begun Jan. 7, 1894, in this paper, is understanding of prosperity, health, irresistible intelligence.

What Today's Lesson Teaches

Today's lesson points the finger of truth to the doctrine of the self-defending principle common to all men without distinction of color, race, previous condition, or present misery. It is never too late to turn the eye of mind toward the indecomposable, never absent element flowing its changeless course through it. The "I am that I am" is in all men alike. Moses acknowledged it forever; Napoleon for only a time.

"Look unto me, all ye ends of the earth:" "Fear thou not for I am with thee:" "Whatsoever is born of

God overcometh the world." "Now is the accepted time;" "Lo! I am with you always:" "Whosoever will let him come:" "Ye are all kings after the order if Melchisedek," or the right principle.

All the miracles of the world have been performed by those who in some measure felt the reality of their own inward being. They were not imitating outward performances, but acting from interior spirit. This spirit when attended unto constantly makes itself manifest more and more. Moses spent four years in meditation of it, and then saw an acacia bush burning with a smokeless flame and heard a voice plainly speaking forth what operations he should betake himself to.

He was to utilize all his Egyptian learning and military skill in leading his people out of Egypt.

No greater task could have been set a man in that age. It was the very height of improbability that Egypt would give up her two million slaves who were doing their work without recompense. Moses himself saw the immensity of the task. It made him exceedingly meek. Once in pride he had attempted to help the Jews and had to flee for his life. His learning and skill had not saved him or his people. Now in meekness he must take them out safely and be safe himself.

The Safety of Moses

The promised safety of himself is the surest possible token of a wonderful understanding of the power of the divine principle he had been studying so many years. It has been noted of the mystics of all ages that they were exceedingly doubtful of their own personal safety in carrying out great undertakings. Most of them expected martyrdom and got it. Not because it was necessary or sure to overtake a man espousing a feeling principle, but because the changeless of the protecting power has not struck their attention.

A man who gets imprisoned or sown asunder for telling a truth or performing a miracle of truth is more like Napoleon than Frederick. Personal safety is the surest evidence of a good understanding of God. Moses heard the voice of the "I Am that I Am" actually promising. *"Certainly I will be with thee. And I will stretch out my hand and smite Egypt with all my wonders, which I will do in the midst thereof, and after that he will let you go."*

And Moses said he was not able to do all that was asked of him, except the mighty arm upheld him, and by a new order of miracle-working loosed the hand of Egypt from the throat of Israel. Then followed miracle after miracle.

In our day we are aware what makes so many millions of beggars. We know how it is that while the earth throws up her rich harvests and the barns and granaries are over full, the multitudes are hungry and unclothed.

All this time we see that there are mystic watchers in the Horeb mountains, who, as one man, are touching the secret springs of a freedom such as never was demonstrated upon the earth.

Man is to be set free from supposing that the omnipotent principle he has hitherto called God needs any assistance from him in brave deeds of able men.

All the mystic thinkers in the Horeb mountains of this hour hear the voice from the smokeless fire on the Sinai top of their lonely thinking proclaiming that we are set free from responsibility in the matter of helping our fellow men out of this universal claim to the bondage of poverty, debt, idleness, which represented by the story of Moses leading a multitude out of the clutches of an Egypt in the year 1493 B.C. wholly and entirely by the power of his own "I Am that I Am" relied upon, while he did nothing, not even having acting faith in it, not having any boldness, not eager to help, fully aware of the overwhelming superiority of Egypt over the flimsy slaves of his age, whose only apparent signs were their multiplication, their ignorant unrest, and their prayers.

Moses brought no bravery to the situation. He brought no eloquence. He brought a few writings which some of the slaves read. He brought his ability to keep his eye on that everlasting stream of self-existent purpose coursing its way through him. That was all.

Whoever thinks he has to raise an army, incite a riot, preach a sermon, write a book, condemn the age or systems thereof, let him study the plan of Moses. Let him turn his gaze toward that underlying eternal flow at the foundations of his being. He will find that its message is now, as it forever - was: *"I will bring you up out of the afflictions of Egypt."*

Inter-Ocean Newspaper, May 27, 1894

LESSON X

The Passover Instituted

Exodus 12:1-14

The ancient natives called the land of Egypt "Kem," which means "black soil." The Greeks first named it "Egypt." The Hebrews called it Nisraim. The Hieroglyphics on the monuments of their undated past still firmly insist upon "Kem" as the rightful name of that country, whose history goes farther back than that of any other people.

"Black soil" — fertile darkness, science, art, literature, wealth, with unrepeated perfectness, flourished under the dispensation of profound materiality of mind. At its highest point of dominion there arose a religious sect proclaiming that there is a principle of life by which mind may conduct itself that man need not be under the dominion of his neighbor; man need not learn of his neighbor; man need not depend upon his neighbor. Each, man shall have himself to his own dominion; his own understanding; his own friendship; his own support.

When such a principle sounds its note amid the clang of machinery and clash of employer and employed, as they daze and phase a world with their din, there are always sure to be a Moses, Aaron, and Miriam arise as the principle bloom of the religious sect. Moses, the meek and self-depreciating, whose one fault is that when he gets self-assertive it is so foreign to his nature that he does not perform it skillfully in the sight of the people; Aaron, who being eloquent and greatly enlightened on the principles proclaimed by his sect, gets easily into the mind of thinking it shows greatness to sit much in judgment. Miriam, who, though understanding the majesty of the hour and the disinterested fidelity of Moses, falls in with cheap grievances and sits in as heavy judgment as her nature will permit. Such, in brief, are the descriptions given of the three Jews who best understood the pristine doctrine of the relation of man to life in the hour of history when the materiality of Kem had two million spiritually inclined people by the neck.

The Exodus a Valuable Forecast

There is no need of disputing whether the story of the exodus of the Jews in the time of Pharaoh is true history or not, the fact remains that if we watch the progress of that whole state of affairs and define each character's performance we can see the invariable and un-deviating conduct of nations and men :in all ages.

That which happened to the Jews and Egyptians 1491 B.C. is happening to a world and religious body 1894 A.D. History in moral is forever repeating itself on a large or small scale. Today the scale is large, covering the entire planet, thus marking the close of the dominion of intellect, the winding up of material history, the end of the world.

Today it is not one man who is Moses; it is all those who are placed in front ranks unwillingly who would gladly live in obscurity, but by reason of their genuine spirituality get mighty revelations who take the Moses position in pure doctrine.

It is not one man who is Aaron, it is all those who are able to speak vividly what they believe, who are enlightened in pure doctrine. It is not one Miriam alone, it is all who have wide, clear understanding and whose preaching of pure doctrine is sweet, like singing with an instrument.

These know that there is one language that has been speaking through the universe from the beginning, which whosoever will hear may hear, and by hearing shall know his way out of sin, sickness, death, poverty, debt, ignorance, old age, delay, misunderstanding, misfortune, inferiority; out of fear of these conditions, out of the very memory of them, out of conditioned existence into unconditioned being, which is out of matter and intellect with their regulations into unregulated God.

What the Unblemished Lamb Typifies

The section of religious story which Moses swings as a censor before us to show out the language of spirit in parable on the question of sacrifice and punishment is found in (Exodus 12:1-4.)

"And the Lord spake unto Moses and Aaron in the land of Egypt saying: 'This month shall be unto you the beginning of the year ... Take a lamb without blemish and sacrifice it ... For I shall pass through the land of Egypt this night and will smite all the first born in the land of Egypt, and against all the gods of Egypt I will execute judgment. I am the Lord.'"

The "unblemished lamb" typifies the purest doctrine we have ever subscribed to; the one we have been most cherishing. On that day when we are most enlightened on the religions of all time and are most meek to receive the language that has always been speaking through the universe we shall see that we do not believe in our doctrine at its very best. It does not express the truth. It must be sacrificed, given up, slain as our crowning error.

The language that speaks through the universe then first finds free transit through us. We are not, then, distracted by the claims of what we have been believing.

Material conditions and the dictations of intellect have us as much in their grasp while we are mesmerized to our religion as while we are mesmerized to our opium.

To throw aside our best doctrine as error at its noblest swing is as much our freedom of spirit as throwing aside our opium or absinthe is our bodily freedom.

Sacrifice always Costly

Whoever lets go of absinthe while he loves it greatly sacrifices it that he may be bodily unencumbered. Whoever lets go of his religion while he loves it greatly sacrifices it that he may be spiritually unencumbered.

"Let us lay aside the weight and the sin that doth beset us."

There is no weight like a pet doctrine, without flaw in its reasoning. There is no sin like a beautiful religion, quoting texts to thrill our heartstrings. They are at their divinest utterance only symbols of that which is being spoken.

The Lord told Moses the divinely disappointed and Aaron the enlightened, that the Jews must eat that sacrifice in haste with their shoes on to run with and their staff in hand to rest with, for when the wailing of Egypt should begin, Israel must be fled out of Kem forever.

So those who now realize that there is somewhat going on through this world which, though set going by the secret conflict of religion with material dominion no religion now proclaimed can live in the face of, sacrifice their religion, and are ready to run whithersoever "the word of the Lord" shall tell them.

For let it be understood that the Lord is present among us, and the Lord hath a language of his own, and they that hear him sacrifice the best they have, which is their faith, or their doctrine, and that is the morning when their freedom dawns in which those who hold hard by their interest in the former things shall not share. And whosoever waileth, he it is that will not sacrifice his theories, his sciences, his religions, to run unencumbered as free mind where the wonderful speech of this mystic hour telleth.

It is not Moses, the believer in miracles that leadeth out. It is the Lord. It is not Aaron that speaketh true doctrines. It is the word of the Lord that worketh and its language is not like the speech of man, neither is its way with the world to be declared save by prototypes like as in this chapter.

Inter-Ocean Newspaper, June 3, 1894

LESSON XI

Passage of the Red Sea

Exodus 14:19-29

Science is the pillar of cloud by day and the pillar of fire by night to show earth's travelers the way to happiness.

The best science for this purpose is not the science of arithmetic, of astronomy, music, war, etc., but the science of light. Moses was learned in all these; but, though he made desperate attempts to get himself and his people free by what he knew of them, he utterly failed. A thorough training in the science of light made him mysteriously competent. Very unusual phenomena were continually taking place wherever Moses appeared after he understood the science of light.

All the phenomena that transpire about any one are compelled by the science he uses. We do not believe there were ever any such living beings as Minerva and Aesculapius, but Aristides the Just, an Athenian leader, 490 B.C., was often visited by them and received personal advices from them concerning his health and military movements.

We do not believe there was ever such a living being as Satan, but he appeared to Martin Luther face to face. There are some very wise men who have concluded there were never any historic characters as Moses and Elias, but Peter and James and John saw them plainly. There are those who do not believe there was ever such a man on earth as Jesus Christ, but even now he appears in persona to multitudes of Christians.

Aristides and Luther Contrasted

Aristides studied the science of invisible people and how to make them visible. Luther studied Satan and his habits, analyzing and comparing till he could call him up any time. Christians study a personal man's life and times, walking him around Galilee, rowing him asleep across waters, and blowing a radiant wind of healing through his body. They oppose regular theology to his spiritual revelations, render doctors of philosophy and medicine insanely jealous of his knowledge and miracles, and finally send him up into the skies with a promise of descending again in like manner. The consequence is that a personal Jesus must as surely appear sometimes to Christians as a personal Minerva to Aristides. The Methodists and Presbyterians discover him pointing a warning finger toward a fire pit, the Catholics see him with thorns and divine anguish of countenance, forever remembering the crucifixion day; the Universalists triumphantly witness him bearing the last sinner into Paradise, washed white as wool.

To those who do not understand trigonometry the strange characters thereof are darkness indeed. To the workman who could not read Latin the sentences they were painting in memorial hall at Harvard University were inartistic scrawls.

The Error of the Egyptians

To the Egyptians the science of the Jews was foolishness. In the figurative language used in today's section of object lessons (Exodus 14:19-29) it was "*a cloud of darkness to them, but it gave light by night to the camp of Israel.*" The science of light preached by Jesus Christ made him to the Jews a stumbling block, and to the Greeks foolishness.

Take the impersonal principles of his science as they are now proclaimed and they will open a man's eyes to see that phenomena are only the tally of his studies. If he has studied the universal splendor that has been called lord of all he will have daily and hourly evidences of some supermental presence. Mind at its best human stretch can not conceive what glories the unknowable light can reveal. By the study of Æsculapius and Minerva Aristides wrought miracles. By the study of Satan and Jesus side by side Gassner wrought miracles. By the study of the light as glorious kindness and wisdom Moses wrought miracles. By the study of the light as Logos or the spoken word of life and love the Christian Scientists work miracles.

Therefore David said, "With all thy getting get understanding." "For wisdom is with him that hath understanding," "and they that understand among the people shall be wise and do exploits."

One glare of the science of the Lord, as Moses declared it, showed the Egyptians that there was no use fighting them. (Verse 24) One instant of understanding the science which the Christians called "scientists" are walking by, would show all the other religionists of the world that it is composed of their own supermost and most splendid teachings which they had ignored. They would see that we might as well strike at the midnight stars with pine sticks as to strike at the people who walk in its light. (Verve 25)

The Christian Life Not Easy

A religionist walking by the silence of the personal Jesus says: "A really earnest and faithful Christian life never gets easy." (International Notes by Peloubet, p.77.) By the flash of one text from the impersonal Christ what would he be dismayed to see? *"My yoke is easy and my burden is light."* Another writes poetry for the same page which says:

"We rise by the things that are under feet;
  By what we have mastered of good and gain;

By the pride deposed and the passion slain;
  And the vanquished ills that we hourly meet."

What says the science of light on the subject of pride, passion, greed, pain? "There is only God, who knoweth all there is to know but knoweth not these things; therefore they do not exist, and we need not try to put them under feet. We are not called upon to contend with straws." "All thy ways are pleasantness and all thy paths are peace."

We can make out a science of anything. If we have a science of warfare as far advanced as the Egyptians in the time of the exodus, for a guide on the path of happiness, we will have lifted a brazen grate filled with fire borne ahead of our army on its marches.

If we have a science of warfare as advanced as the Jews of that date, we shall find the light by night unkindled by human fingers. If we have a science of warfare as brilliant as the truth will permit, we shall have a joyous, speedy journey into the haven we are all asking for. We shall know no enemies, encounter none.

The Wisdom of the Schools

As the human army marches heavenward at this hour we see certain of them making up a science of worms and competitions which they carry aloft to cheer themselves onward with. We call it material science, but the scriptures tell us it is *"falsely so called."* (I Timothy 6:20) We call it the wisdom of the schools, but the science of light shows plainly that it is "foolishness with God." Some are making up a science of mind and showing how mind causes pain of body, disasters in business, old age, death, and weeping. It is a science which would deceive the very elect, for the Bibles of the world seem to agree with it.

Do we not read that for the lightest word we shall give account?

It would verily seem by this law that the earth would cease to revolve if Galileo should say that it did not do so. But as the earth revolved just the same whatever Galileo said about it, so the true science reads that no man changes anything by what he does or says. He only sees what is going on around him according to his science which he has made up.

There has been a science of safety instituted among men for the overcoming of opposition forces by brave efforts. This lesson of the Jewish safety, with its mystic meaning, shows that we are to run away from the things that beset us if we have the true light ahead of us.

The True Light Explained

The true light ahead is the science of safety by yielding every point to every enemy we have. Let the rocks alone if they do not build your house without your brave struggle against their nature. Your vision will thus be clearer to see your mansion close at hand, which was prepared from the beginning, and no tired father climbed ladders to dizzy heights to tip its roof points with the wondrous light that streams forever from it.

If people refuse to 'do the right' by you let them do their own way unrebuked. With your mind on the true light they will disappear out of your horizon. (Verse 28) The true light is the light that teaches for its principle truth that the less you do for yourself the more you will see that is already done for you. It would be a shame if truth needed to be fought for, worked for, or quarreled for. Knowing what the truth is, keep your eyes on it as the two million Jews watched the pillar of fire, and see it do its own fighting.

"I will make her that halted a strong nation."

By no process whatsoever can anybody get anything whatsoever away from you while your mind's eye is fixed on the science that asks no assistance of anybody to drown, and strangle everything and every body that opposes you while you are studying it. (Verse 29)

Whatever is chasing you up, whether sorrow, want, deafness, blindness, competitors for your place, unmanageable disposition, or the whole of them together, while your study of the true science is claiming your attention, they shall never reach you. They shall dissolve if they are near you.

Had the Jews stopped to have a brave fight they had not told us this glad lesson. Martyrdom for truth is the wisdom of darkness. The new science is "I will fight for them."

Inter-Ocean Newspaper, June 10, 1894

LESSON XII

The Woes Of The Drunkard

Proverbs 23:29-35

It is written of Jonah that while he was yet incased in the whale's dark dungeon he kept his mind's eye on the temple of Jerusalem, standing in glistening beauty and still with the noon sunshine intensifying its blended splendors of white and gold.

This sight drew him out of the whale into the free air. Had he looked around him and described the gloom of his environments he had never arrived on the banks of the Mediterranean to tell the law of Plato,

"That thou seest,

That thou beest."

Today's lesson being called a "temperance" one, with the real intention to find a reform for too much alcoholic imbibing, we must take careful note of what the inspired of all time have taught as sure cure.

We will take Jonah's situation as identical with the profound darkness of the bondage to drink as described by our accepted teachers. Could there be a darker picture of the power of a material thing over a man's will than this paragraph from the Sunday-school notes, page 173: "in spite of all warnings and in the face of all consequences, the drunkard returns again to his cups. Put wife and children in the path before him and he casts them aside. Put respectability and honor and manhood there; they gaze at them a moment and fling them away. Bring heaven and Christ and salvation to withstand their downward way and they trample them under their feet. Lay remorse with all its coiling serpent tongues and scorpion stings in their path, yet they walk on. Pile up miseries, sorrows, pains, diseases before them, yea, point out in the way the ghastly form of death, and they still go on, for they will have rum."

Now far be it from any man to give so little power to "heaven and Christ and salvation," and so much power to a keg of fluid.

Heaven and Christ Will Help

On another round of the spiral it is Jonah giving all power to the walls of his dungeon, and no power to the Temple of Jerusalem.

If "heaven and Christ and salvation" don't work when they are presented to a man in dark chains it is because they are less vividly portrayed than the dark chains.

When a man or woman wants to reform a neighbor what does he or she persistently do? Why, describe the miseries and horrors of drink, of course — and keep it up, and keep it up till the picture is as natural as experience.

The warrior who can paint the terrors of the coming campaign most vividly rouses most men to his regiments. It was the pride of France that her soldiers were "heroes in rags." Religion has howled on her millions with the promise of "cold and hunger, rags and death."

"Martyrdom painted oft,

Familiar with her face,

We first endure,

Then pity, then embrace."

So the preachers have gone on from Solomon to the modern Sunday-school teachers rousing the heroism of our youth, till on page 85 of the lesson notes we are shown the triumphs of darkness, as an expenditure of over $1,000,000,000 for alcohol in the United States in one year.

There is something fascinating in pictures of hardship and suffering to the ardent strength of the young. But there is something infinitely more enchanting in pictures of wisdom and majesty and exposures of the divinity inherent in all men. If Jonah's mind's eye on a glorified temple drew him by its mystic chains into freedom, the young man's mental eye, fastened on the majesty and grandeur of his own native character, shall land him on the shores of the continent where the mighty beings walk who never assumed the lies of man's feebleness, but who are fit comrades to his noblest dreams of greatness.

The Woes of the Drunkard

The subject of today's lesson is taken from Proverbs 23:29-35, and is called "The Woes of the Drunkard." This is the picture today being held up for millions of boys and girls, men and women, to flinch under. The picture is vivid. The power of darkness is described with a success of eloquence and pain that wore the swift; flight of our wondrous soul into the glorious liberty of the sons of God if employed in describing man's transcendent heart of goodness.

"Had I but serv'd my God with half the zeal

I serv'd my king he would not in my age

Have left me naked to my enemies."

Alcohol is called king by temperance reformers. How splendid a war to wage if I go out to fight a mighty king! The more powerful my antagonist the greater my prowess! I could find no temptation to fight "King Alcohol" if he were painted as a puny vanity. I must test myself in his clutches, is the unconscious reasoning of mind.

The series of questions put from verse 29 to verse 30, about who hath woe, sorrow, contention, etc., is answered by "they that tarry long at the wine." Now, in all scripture "wine" has metaphysical or symbolic meanings. It means human will and divine will. Whoever tarries at the cup of having his own will whether or no, has exactly the experiences here described. Martin Luther said he would march to Leipzig if it rained on Duke George nine days running. He could not possibly recognize that Duke George might have some rights in the case.

The Fight Still Continues

His ideas of the lion and the lamb lying down together was with the undigested lamb inside the lion. He fought Catholicism to eat it up root and branch. And they fought him for the like purpose. What was the consequence? The Roman Catholics and Protestants, even on our Chicago streets, are "still at it." The question Solomon asks is thus answered. "Who hath contentions?" They that will have their say anyhow. So they that will describe the power of rum have for their statistics "the awful increase of intoxication?"

Mohammed said if the sun stood on one hand and the moon on the other he would go and preach — what? Why, that "Jo hoga so hoga." And that a man might not rob a believer but might rob a stranger, that he was the greatest prophet ever sent from God, and that poor Moses was whimpering with envy in the third heaven. How now? The unbelievers are still contending with Mohammed's followers.

"Take now a little wine," said Paul. A little of the divine will — a very little taste will work wonders! "Jo hoga so hoga" means "What will be will be." Do you not see that if this text of Mohammed's own doctrine were true he need not slam around and stab strangers to establish the power of God?

The Society of Friends

Could Moses be whimpering with envy who had for his principles of warfare "The Lord will fight for you, and ye shall hold your peace?" The Sun and moon, with their everlasting protest against the claims of darkness, had some rights.

There is one class of people only dwelling upon the earth who have never carried outer arms of contention and very little power in description of wickedness. They are the Quakers. Everybody loves and respects them. They walked safely between the armies of the North and the South in the days of the rebellion. They thought more of the indwelling will of God than of the claims of bondage. The North would fight with guns and sabers and the South would fight with sabers and guns. They would have each side their will. So the North and South are still at variance. The lion lieth down with the undigested lamb still grumbling. Why? Because of tarrying long at the wine of human will. One taste of the divine will is one sight of the majesty and wonder of God. Every man springeth thereby to his undefeatable liberty.

Freedom that is bought with bloodshed is not freedom. Temperance that is bought with warfare on rum is not temperance. The kingdom of greatness, majesty, power, cometh with watching it. The greatness, wisdom, beauty of man come forward by vivid portrayals. Emerson said the young man is a demigod, but Jesus Christ proves he is all God.

Inter-Ocean Newspaper, June 17, 1894

LESSON XIII

REVIEW

The ancient Chinese had a theory that the sons of Paradise descended to this earth, and getting lost among its shadows, forgot their way home. After a time an angel came and cut off all the lines of communication between the country from which they came forth and the earth country, and since that there have been only vague and indistinct memories in the breasts of the Elohim concerning their native Paradise.

When the lines upon which they might have ascended and descended as the angels on Jacob's ladder were cut off then all knowledge became the wisdom of foolishness and all actions became vanity upon this globe.

We study botany, picking apart blossoms and roots, but cannot study the intelligence and life that smile in our faces while we are counting stamens and pistils. The language of communication between that smile and the mind of man is cut off, leaving that school-book wisdom a lifeless, smileless, heartless jargon.

Paul said: *"The wisdom of the fools is foolishness with God."* We study astronomy, naming the constellations and defining the planets but know not the scheme of the wondrous mind that attends so majestically to its own handiwork, touching our faces and fingers at every turn but communicating no message of dominion.

"Canst, thou loose the bands of Orion?

Canst thou bind the sweet influences of the Pleiades?"

Can the learned men stop the tidal wave that they prophesy to submerge New York this summer, or stay the comet's clash against our planet, which they predict will shortly come to pass?

"What power can stay it in its onward course?

Or melt its iron heart to pity?"

Where Is Man's Dominion?

The word that streamed through the universe at the starting point of man was: "Let us make man and let him have dominion." But where is that dominion? Somebody or something has dominion.

The Hebrews and Hindus in most ancient days said that there is a way of remembering great men's high teachings about the starting point from whence all things spring till we all might remember and remember the bright home from whence we took our flight.

"For not in utter nakedness,

Or all forgetfulness,

Did we come

From God who is our home."

The primal purpose of religious recitation was to recite mind's way back into Paradise. The Chinese promised that some day the stairway would be opened again. The Hebrews promised one to come who should wholly remember the country from whence we all came out and successfully wake the long slumbered recollection of home in all mankind till there should not be one of us but would utterly return by the shining ladder of his reminders.

When one shows power to do miraculous things simply by his mind alone, we say he remembers a little of his original mind. "When one speaks with enchaining eloquence we say his tongue is tipped with memory of that language of the gods which we all once spoke.

By word or by work Paradise is brought to mind. Aaron could speak with enlightened eloquence; Moses could work miracles. The silent Buddhists do startling works. Their free-spoken comrades touch Western shores a workless crew, but nobody complains because they do nothing but talk, for their speech touches some long-mute chord in their hearers' hearts.

Wrestling of Jacob

Jacob wrestled with his memory of blessedness and dominion over danger till at daybreak he caught it exactly as the mathematician catches the solution to his problem after wrestling with his spirit. Each is wrestling to remember a moiety (a half) of what he knew so well at his starting point.

Joseph wrestled with his memory of wisdom without material perseverance and dominion without warfare. Telling his brethren thereof as a principle before he proved it they sold him into deeper slavery to material ways, just as we set our minds to the determination that if the sons of men do not have money they shall starve, while they are telling of the providing power of the recital of truth before they have proved it.

Striking a utilitarian age, the mere recital of such passages of light as remind mind of its original state will not touch the heart chords of many men, for they will not take time to listen.

The Josephs must serve their thirteen years of knowing that they have a power to feed, enlighten, empower, and beautify themselves without friends and without money before proving their knowledge. The crowds cry, "If thou be the Christ save thyself," for a period of thirteen years, then suddenly Joseph could remember the words of freedom.

He who can recite the right words of the freedom he had as Son of Paradise shall demonstrate freedom. He who is free has princely power. Whoever can now recite the last lines on prosperity and poverty is setting most men's minds on the ladder of liberty. (Genesis 41)

He who can keep most silent while knowing most of the original God in all men is most capable of probing the secret hearts of men, and exposing their native inherent goodness.

When the Man Is Seen

Nobody is fitted to be head of government till his silent knowledge of the original heart of man is so great that like Joseph melting the eleven criminals he melts the criminal classes into unity with his mind. (Genesis 45)

Lao Tzu said: "They who know do not talk, they who talk do not yet know." When once the mortal quality is touched the man that was born of God begins to be seen. When the man that is born of God is seen his multiplying and replenishing power springs up. (Exodus 1) We know this by remembering the story of the Israelites in this call for a review of spiritual teachings, (International series, p. 174)

"Whatsoever is born of God overcometh the world." Even bread that a Joseph knows the truth about will touch its God origin and multiply to feed whomsoever a chief of affairs of the right order shall decree. John Grande, in the year 1579, took a small piece of bread and meat and multiplied it to feed a mass of starving poor by knowing how to place the slices in the line of their God starting point. So did the Jesuit, Francis Regis, about the year 1635. So did the Jews multiply when Joseph put them into recollection of their birth from God.

So did not the Egyptians when they had a king over them who knew not Joseph. The Egyptian king now is this world-wide ignorance of how to make bread and clothing, wisdom, and love increase by putting them into the straight line of their origin.

Oh, there is a way to lay your singing voice into lines with its starting point and beautifying it till it overcometh the world. There is a way to put your fingers on the God nigh their trembling touches to make them as skillful as Jehovah's.

Set much store by the "borning" from God which all actions must lay hold of. Pay attention to laying your mind into line with recitals of the wonders of the mind it started from. That wonderful mind is not far away. It is nigh us all. This is the new age, the millennial time, which urges us to notice more how all things started in Paradise and may return thither. This is the Moses principle born to our age. It is a truth which will rust the gold of the banker in its vaults, for whosoever knows it can take care of himself without that kind of gold. (Exodus 14)

It is a truth which takes away all the former religious teachings about "the nations that have forgotten God," about the "cry of the poor," the "unrest of the world," and the "injustice of man with man." My words are born of God, my actions are born of God, my bread is born of God, my clothes are born of God.

"Heaven opens wide her ever-during gates.

Harmonious sound on golden hinges moving."

The lesson notes tell us to have for our recital of the steps back to our happy home these fourteen, viz.: "Afflicted, hardened, sold, blood, I am, wages, dream, overthrew, wept, east wind, passover, wrestled, famine, plague," but the spirit of memory, stirring mind, causes it to recite to its fourteen conditions the everlasting truth, "Born of God, born of God."

Inter-Ocean Newspaper, June 24, 1894

Notes

Other Books by Emma Curtis Hopkins

- *Class Lessons of 1888 (WiseWoman Press)*
- *Bible Interpretations (WiseWoman Press)*
- *Esoteric Philosophy in Spiritual Science (WiseWoman Press)*
- *Genesis Series*
- *High Mysticism (WiseWoman Press)*
- *Self Treatments with Radiant I Am (WiseWoman Press)*
- *Gospel Series (WiseWoman Press)*
- *Judgment Series in Spiritual Science (WiseWoman Press)*
- *Drops of Gold (WiseWoman Press)*
- *Resume (WiseWoman Press)*
- *Scientific Christian Mental Practice (DeVorss)*

Books about Emma Curtis Hopkins and her teachings

- *Emma Curtis Hopkins, Forgotten Founder of New Thought* – Gail Harley
- *Unveiling Your Hidden Power: Emma Curtis Hopkins' Metaphysics for the 21st Century (also as a Workbook and as A Guide for Teachers)* – Ruth L. Miller
- *Power to Heal: Easy reading biography for all ages* –Ruth Miller

To find more of Emma's work, including some previously unpublished material, log on to:

www.highwatch.org

www.emmacurtishopkins.com

WISEWOMAN PRESS

1408 NE 65th St.
Vancouver, WA 98665
800.603.3005
www.wisewomanpress.com

Books Published by WiseWoman Press

By Emma Curtis Hopkins

- *Resume*
- *Gospel Series*
- *Class Lessons of 1888*
- *Self Treatments including Radiant I Am*
- *High Mysticism*
- *Esoteric Philosophy in Spiritual Science*
- *Drops of Gold Journal*
- *Judgment Series*
- *Bible Interpretations: Series I, thru XII*

By Ruth L. Miller

- *Unveiling Your Hidden Power: Emma Curtis Hopkins' Metaphysics for the 21st Century*
- *Coming into Freedom: Emily Cady's Lessons in Truth for the 21st Century*
- *150 Years of Healing: The Founders and Science of New Thought*
- *Power Beyond Magic: Ernest Holmes Biography*
- *Power to Heal: Emma Curtis Hopkins Biography*
- *The Power of Unity: Charles Fillmore Biography*
- *Power of Thought: Phineas P. Quimby Biography*
- *Gracie's Adventures with God*
- *Uncommon Prayer*
- *Spiritual Success*
- *Finding the Path*

Watch our website for release dates and order information! - www.wisewomanpress.com

List of Bible Interpretation Series with date from 1st to 14th Series.

This list is complete through the fourteenth Series. Emma produced at least thirty Series of Bible Interpretations.

She followed the Bible Passages provided by the International Committee of Clerics who produced the Bible Quotations for each year's use in churches all over the world.

Emma used these for her column of Bible Interpretations in both the Christian Science Magazine, at her Seminary and in the Chicago Inter-Ocean Newspaper.

First Series

July 5 - September 27, 1891

Lesson 1	The Word Made Flesh	July 5th
	John 1:1-18	
Lesson 2	Christ's First Disciples	July 12th
	John 1:29-42	
Lesson 3	All Is Divine Order	July 19th
	*John 2:1-1*1 (Christ's first Miracle)	
Lesson 4	Jesus Christ and Nicodemus	July 26th
	John 3:1-17	
Lesson 5	Christ at Samaria	August 2nd
	John 4:5-26 (Christ at Jacob's Well)	
Lesson 6	Self-condemnation	August 9th
	John 5:17-30 (Christ's Authority)	
Lesson 7	Feeding the Starving	August 16th
	John 6:1-14 (The Five Thousand Fed)	
Lesson 8	The Bread of Life	August 23rd
	John 6:26-40 (Christ the Bread of Life)	
Lesson 9	The Chief Thought	August 30th
	John 7:31-34 (Christ at the Feast)	
Lesson 10	Continue the Work	September 6th
	John 8:31-47	
Lesson 11	Inheritance of Sin	September 13th
	John 9:1-11, 35-38 (Christ and the Blind Man)	
Lesson 12	The Real Kingdom	September 20th
	John 10:1-16 (Christ the Good Shepherd)	
Lesson 13	In Retrospection	September 27th
		Review

Second Series

October 4 - December 27, 1891

Lesson 1	Mary and Martha *John 11:21-44*	October 4th
Lesson 2	Glory of Christ *John 12:20-36*	October 11th
Lesson 3	Good in Sacrifice *John 13:1-17*	October 18th
Lesson 4	Power of the Mind *John 14:13; 15-27*	October 25th
Lesson 5	Vines and Branches *John 15:1-16*	November 1st
Lesson 6	Your Idea of God *John 16:1-15*	November 8th
Lesson 7	Magic of His Name *John 17:1-19*	November 15th
Lesson 8	Jesus and Judas *John 18:1-13*	November 22nd
Lesson 9	Scourge of Tongues *John 19:1-16*	November 29th
Lesson 10	Simplicity of Faith *John 19:17-30*	December 6th
Lesson 11	Christ is All in All *John 20: 1-18*	December 13th
Lesson 12	Risen With Christ *John 21:1-14*	December 20th
Lesson 13	The Spirit is Able Review of Year	December 27th

Third Series

January 3 - March 27, 1892

Lesson 1	A Golden Promise *Isaiah 11:1-10*	January 3rd
Lesson 2	The Twelve Gates *Isaiah 26:1-10*	January 10th
Lesson 3	Who Are Drunkards *Isaiah 28:1-13*	January 17th
Lesson 4	Awake Thou That Sleepest *Isaiah 37:1-21*	January 24th
Lesson 5	The Healing Light *Isaiah 53:1-21*	January 31st
Lesson 6	True Ideal of God *Isaiah 55:1-13*	February 7th
Lesson 7	Heaven Around Us *Jeremiah 31 14-37*	February 14th
Lesson 8	But One Substance *Jeremiah 36:19-31*	February 21st
Lesson 9	Justice of Jehovah *Jeremiah 37:11-21*	February 28th
Lesson 10	God and Man Are One *Jeremiah 39:1-10*	March 6th
Lesson 11	Spiritual Ideas *Ezekiel 4:9, 36:25-38*	March 13th
Lesson 12	All Flesh is Grass *Isaiah 40:1-10*	March 20th
Lesson 13	The Old and New Contrasted Review	March 27th

Fourth Series

April 3 - June 26, 1892

Lesson 1	Realm of Thought *Psalm 1:1-6*	April 3rd
Lesson 2	The Power of Faith *Psalm 2:1-12*	April 10th
Lesson 3	Let the Spirit Work *Psalm 19:1-14*	April 17th
Lesson 4	Christ is Dominion *Psalm 23:1-6*	April 24th
Lesson 5	External or Mystic *Psalm 51:1-13*	May 1st
Lesson 6	Value of Early Beliefs *Psalm 72: 1-9*	May 8th
Lesson 7	Truth Makes Free *Psalm 84:1-12*	May 15th
Lesson 8	False Ideas of God *Psalm 103:1-22*	May 22nd
Lesson 9	But Men Must Work *Daniel 1:8-21*	May 29th
Lesson 10	Artificial Helps *Daniel 2:36-49*	June 5th
Lesson 11	Dwelling in Perfect Life *Daniel 3:13-25*	June 12th
Lesson 12	Which Streak Shall Rule *Daniel 6:16-28*	June 19th
Lesson 13	See Things as They Are Review of 12 Lessons	June 26th

Fifth Series

July 3 - September 18, 1892

Lesson 1	The Measure of a Master *Acts 1:1-12*	July 3rd
Lesson 2	Chief Ideas Rule People *Acts 2:1-12*	July 10th
Lesson 3	New Ideas About Healing *Acts 2:37-47*	July 17th
Lesson 4	Heaven a State of Mind *Acts 3:1-16*	July 24th
Lesson 5	About Mesmeric Powers *Acts 4:1-18*	July 31st
Lesson 6	Points in the Mosaic Law *Acts 4:19-31*	August 7th
Lesson 7	Napoleon's Ambition *Acts 5:1-11*	August 14th
Lesson 8	A River Within the Heart *Acts 5:25-41*	August 21st
Lesson 9	The Answering of Prayer Acts 7: 54-60 - Acts 8: 1-4	August 28th
Lesson 10	Words Spoken by the Mind *Acts 8:5-35*	September 4th
Lesson 11	Just What It Teaches Us *Acts 8:26-40*	September 11th
Lesson 12	The Healing Principle Review	September 18th

Sixth Series

September 25 - December 18, 1892

Lesson 1	The Science of Christ *1 Corinthians 11:23-34*	September 25th
Lesson 2	On the Healing of Saul *Acts 9:1-31*	October 2nd
Lesson 3	The Power of the Mind Explained *Acts 9:32-43*	October 9th
Lesson 4	Faith in Good to Come *Acts 10:1-20*	October 16th
Lesson 5	Emerson's Great Task *Acts 10:30-48*	October 23rd
Lesson 6	The Teaching of Freedom *Acts 11:19-30*	October 30th
Lesson 7	Seek and Ye Shall Find *Acts 12:1-17*	November 6th
Lesson 8	The Ministry of the Holy Mother *Acts 13:1-13*	November 13th
Lesson 9	The Power of Lofty Ideas *Acts 13:26-43*	November 20th
Lesson 10	Sure Recipe for Old Age *Acts 13:44-52, 14:1-7*	November 27th
Lesson 11	The Healing Principle *Acts 14:8-22*	December 4th
Lesson 12	Washington's Vision *Acts 15:12-29*	December 11th
Lesson 13	Review of the Quarter	December 18th
Partial Lesson	Shepherds and the Star	December 25th

Seventh Series

January 1 - March 31, 1893

Lesson 1	All is as Allah Wills	January 1st
	Ezra 1	
	Khaled Knew that he was of The Genii	
	The Coming of Jesus	
Lesson 2	Zerubbabel's High Ideal	January 8th
	Ezra 2:8-13	
	Fulfillments of Prophecies	
	Followers of the Light	
	Doctrine of Spinoza	
Lesson 3	Divine Rays Of Power	January 15th
	Ezra 4	
	The Twelve Lessons of Science	
Lesson 4	Visions Of Zechariah	January 22nd
	Zechariah 3	
	Subconscious Belief in Evil	
	Jewish Ideas of Deity	
	Fruits of Mistakes	
Lesson 5	Aristotle's Metaphysician	January 27th
	Missing (See Review for summary)	
Lesson 6	The Building of the Temple	February 3rd
	Missing (See Review for summary)	
Lesson 7	Pericles and his Work in building the Temple	
	Nehemiah 13	February 12th
	Supreme Goodness	
	On and Upward	
Lesson 8	Ancient Religions	February 19th
	Nehemiah 1	
	The Chinese	
	The Holy Spirit	
Lesson 9	Understanding is Strength Part 1	February 26th
	Nehemiah 13	
Lesson 10	Understanding is Strength Part 2	March 3rd
	Nehemiah 13	
Lesson 11	Way of the Spirit	March 10th
	Esther	
Lesson 12	Speaking of Right Things	March 17th
		Proverbs 23:15-23
Lesson 13	Review	March 24th

Eighth Series

April 2 - June 25, 1893

Lesson 1	The Resurrection *Matthew 28:1-10* One Indestructible Life In Eternal Abundance The Resurrection Shakes Nature Herself Gospel to the Poor	April 2nd
Lesson 2	Universal Energy *Book of Job, Part I*	April 9th
Lesson 3	Strength From Confidence *Book of Job, Part II*	April 16th
Lesson 4	The New Doctrine Brought Out *Book of Job, Part III*	April 23rd
Lesson 5	The Golden Text *Proverbs 1:20-23* Personification Of Wisdom Wisdom Never Hurts The "Two" Theory All is Spirit	April 30th
Lesson 6	The Law of Understanding *Proverbs 3* Shadows of Ideas The Sixth Proposition What Wisdom Promises Clutch On Material Things The Tree of Life Prolonging Illuminated Moments	May 7th
Lesson 7	Self-Esteem *Proverbs 12:1-15* Solomon on Self-Esteem The Magnetism of Passing Events Nothing Established by Wickedness Strength of a Vitalized Mind Concerning the "Perverse Heart"	May 14th

Lesson 8	Physical vs. Spiritual Power	May 21st
	Proverbs 23:29-35	

Law of Life to Elevate the Good and Banish the Bad
Lesson Against Intemperance
Good Must Increase
To Know Goodness Is Life
The Angel of God's Presence

Lesson 9	Lesson missing	May 28th
	(See Review for concept)	
Lesson 10	Recognizing Our Spiritual Nature	June 4th
	Proverbs 31:10-31	

Was Called Emanuel
The covenant of Peace
The Ways of the Divine
Union With the Divine
Miracles Will Be Wrought

Lesson 11	Intuition	June 11th
	Ezekiel 8:2-3	
	Ezekiel 9:3-6, 11	

Interpretation of the Prophet
Ezekiel's Vision
Dreams and Their Cause
Israel and Judah
Intuition the Head
Our Limited Perspective

Lesson 12	The Book of Malachi	June 18th
	Malachi	

The Power of Faith
The Exercise of thankfulness
Her Faith Self-Sufficient
Burned with the Fires of Truth
What is Reality
One Open Road

Lesson 13	Review of the Quarter	June 25th
	Proverbs 31:10-31	

Ninth Series

July 2 - September 27, 1893

Lesson 1	Secret of all Power	July 2nd
Acts 16: 6-15	The Ancient Chinese Doctrine of Taoism	
	Manifesting of God Powers	
	Paul, Timothy, and Silas	
	Is Fulfilling as Prophecy	
	The Inner Prompting.	
	Good Taoist Never Depressed	
Lesson 2	The Flame of Spiritual Verity	July 9th
Acts 16:18	Cause of Contention	
	Delusive Doctrines	
	Paul's History	
	Keynotes	
	Doctrine Not New	
Lesson 3	Healing Energy Gifts	July 16th
Acts 18:19-21	How Paul Healed	
	To Work Miracles	
	Paul Worked in Fear	
	Shakespeare's Idea of Loss	
	Endurance the Sign of Power	
Lesson 4	Be Still My Soul	July 23rd
Acts 17:16-24	Seeing Is Believing	
	Paul Stood Alone	
	Lessons for the Athenians	
	All Under His Power	
	Freedom of Spirit	
Lesson 5	(Missing) Acts 18:1-11	July 30th
Lesson 6	Missing No Lesson *	August 6th
Lesson 7	The Comforter is the Holy Ghost	August 13th
Acts 20	Requisite for an Orator	
	What is a Myth	
	Two Important Points	
	Truth of the Gospel	
	Kingdom of the Spirit	
	Do Not Believe in Weakness	

Lesson 8	Conscious of a Lofty Purpose	August 20th
Acts 21	As a Son of God	
	Wherein Paul failed	
	Must Give Up the Idea	
	Associated with Publicans	
	Rights of the Spirit	
Lesson 9	Measure of Understanding	August 27th
Acts 24:19-32	Lesser of Two Evils	
	A Conciliating Spirit	
	A Dream of Uplifting	
	The Highest Endeavor	
	Paul at Caesarea	
	Preparatory Symbols	
	Evidence of Christianity	
Lesson 10	The Angels of Paul	September 3rd
Acts 23:25-26	Paul's Source of Inspiration	
	Should Not Be Miserable	
	Better to Prevent than Cure	
	Mysteries of Providence	
Lesson 11	The Hope of Israel	September 10th
Acts 28:20-31	Immunity for Disciples	
	Hiding Inferiorities	
	Pure Principle	
Lesson 12	Joy in the Holy Ghost	September 17th
Romans 14	Temperance	
	The Ideal Doctrine	
	Tells a Different Story	
	Hospitals as Evidence	
	Should Trust in the Savior	
Lesson 13	Review	September 24th
Acts 26-19-32	The Leveling Doctrine	
	Boldness of Command	
	Secret of Inheritance	
	Power in a Name	

Tenth Series

October 1 – December 24, 1893

Lesson 1	*Romans 1:1-19* When the Truth is Known Faith in God The Faithful Man is Strong Glory of the Pure Motive	October 1st
Lesson 2	*Romans 3:19-26* Free Grace. On the Gloomy Side Daniel and Elisha Power from Obedience Fidelity to His Name He Is God	October 8th
Lesson 3	*Romans 5* The Healing Principle Knows No Defeat. In Glorified Realms He Will Come	October 15th
Lesson 4	*Romans 12:1* Would Become Free Man's Co-operation Be Not Overcome Sacrifice No Burden Knows the Future	October 22nd
Lesson 5	*I Corinthians 8:1-13* The Estate of Man Nothing In Self What Paul Believed Doctrine of Kurozumi	October 29th
Lesson 6	*I Corinthians 12:1-26* Science of The Christ Principle Dead from the Beginning St. Paul's Great Mission What The Spark Becomes Chris, All There Is of Man Divinity Manifest in Man Christ Principle Omnipotent	November 5th

Lesson 7	*II Corinthians 8:1-12*	November 12th
	Which Shall It Be?	
	The Spirit is Sufficient	
	Working of the Holy Ghost	
Lesson 8	*Ephesians 4:20-32*	November 19th
	A Source of Comfort	
	What Causes Difference of Vision	
	Nothing But Free Will	
Lesson 9	*Colossians 3:12-25*	November 26th
	Divine in the Beginning	
	Blessings of Contentment	
	Free and Untrammeled Energy	
Lesson 10	*James 1*	December 3rd
	The Highest Doctrine	
	A Mantle of Darkness	
	The Counsel of God	
	Blessed Beyond Speaking	
Lesson 11	*I Peter 1*	December 10th
	Message to the Elect	
	Not of the World's Good	
Lesson 12	*Revelation 1:9*	December 17th
	Self-Glorification	
	The All-Powerful Name	
	Message to the Seven Churches	
	The Voice of the Spirit	
Lesson 13	Golden Text	December 24th
	Responding Principle Lives	
	Principle Not Hidebound	
	They Were Not Free Minded	
Lesson 14	Review	December 31st
	It is Never Too Late	
	The Just Live by Faith	
	An Eternal Offer	
	Freedom of Christian Science	

Eleventh Series

January 1 – March 25, 1894

Lesson 1	*Genesis 1:26-31 & 2:1-3*	January 7th
	The First Adam	
	Man: The Image of Language Paul and Elymas	
Lesson 2	*Genesis 3:1-15*	January 14th
	Adam's Sin and God's Grace	
	The Fable of the Garden	
	Looked-for Sympathy	
	The True Doctrine	
Lesson 3	*Genesis 4:3-13*	January 21st
	Types of the Race	
	God in the Murderer	
	God Nature Unalterable	
Lesson 4	*Genesis 9:8-17*	January 28th
	God's Covenant With Noah	
	Value of Instantaneous Action	
	The Lesson of the Rainbow	
Lesson 5	I Corinthians 8:1-13	February 4th
	Genesis 12:1-9	
	Beginning of the Hebrew Nation	
	No Use For Other Themes	
	Influence of Noble Themes	
	Danger In Looking Back	
Lesson 6	*Genesis 17:1-9*	February 11th
	God's Covenant With Abram	
	As Little Children	
	God and Mammon	
	Being Honest With Self	
Lesson 7	*Genesis 18:22-23*	February 18th
	God's Judgment of Sodom	
	No Right Nor Wrong In Truth	
	Misery Shall Cease	
Lesson 8	*Genesis 22:1-13*	February 25th
	Trial of Abraham's Faith	
	Light Comes With Preaching	
	You Can Be Happy NOW	

Lesson 9	*Genesis 25:27-34*	March 4th
	Selling the Birthright	
	"Ye shall be Filled"	
	The Delusion Destroyed	
Lesson 10	*Genesis 28:10-22*	March 11th
	Jacob at Bethel	
	Many Who Act Like Jacob	
	How to Seek Inspiration	
	Christ, the True Pulpit Orator	
	The Priceless Knowledge of God	
Lesson 11	*Proverbs 20:1-7*	March 18th
	Temperance	
	Only One Lord	
	What King Alcohol Does	
	Stupefying Ideas	
Lesson 12	*Mark 16:1-8*	March 25th
	Review and Easter	
	Words of Spirit and Life	
	Facing the Supreme	
	Erasure of the Law	
	Need No Other Friend	

Twelfth Series

April 1 – June 24, 1894

Lesson 1	*Genesis 24:30, 32:09-12*	April 8th
	Jacob's Prevailing Prayer	
	God Transcends Idea	
	All To Become Spiritual	
	Ideas Opposed to Each Other	April 1st
Lesson 2	*Genesis 37:1-11*	
	Discord in Jacob's Family	
	Setting Aside Limitations	
	On the Side of Truth	
Lesson 3	*Genesis 37:23-36*	April 15th
	Joseph Sold into Egypt	
	Influence on the Mind	
	Of Spiritual Origin	
Lesson 4	*Genesis 41:38-48*	April 22nd
	Object Lesson Presented in	
	the Book of Genesis	
Lesson 5	*Genesis 45:1-15*	April 29th
	"With Thee is Fullness of Joy"	
	India Favors Philosophic Thought	
	What These Figures Impart	
	The Errors of Governments	
Lesson 6	*Genesis 50:14-26*	May 6th
	Changes of Heart	
	The Number Fourteen	
	Divine Magicians	
Lesson 7	*Exodus 1:1-14*	May 13th
	Principle of Opposites	
	Power of Sentiment	
	Opposition Must Enlarge	
Lesson 8	*Exodus 2:1-10*	May 20th
	How New Fires Are Enkindled	
	Truth Is Restless	
	Man Started from God	
Lesson 9	*Exodus 3:10-20*	May 27th
	What Science Proves	
	What Today's Lesson Teaches	
	The Safety of Moses	

Lesson 10	*Exodus 12:1-14*	June 3rd
	The Exodus a Valuable Force	
	What the Unblemished Lamp Typifies	
	Sacrifice Always Costly	
Lesson 11	*Exodus 14:19-29*	June 10th
	Aristides and Luther Contrasted	
	The Error of the Egyptians	
	The Christian Life not Easy	
	The True Light Explained	
Lesson 12	*Proverbs 23:29-35*	June 17th
	Heaven and Christ will Help	
	The Woes of the Drunkard	
	The Fight Still Continues	
	The Society of Friends	
Lesson 13	*Proverbs 23:29-35*	June 24th
	Review	
	Where is Man's Dominion	
	Wrestling of Jacob	
	When the Man is Seen	

Thirteenth Series

July 1 – September 30, 1894

Lesson 1	The Birth of Jesus	July 1st
	Luke 2:1-16	
	No Room for Jesus	
	Man's Mystic Center	
	They glorify their Performances	
Lesson 2	Presentation in the Temple	July 8th
	Luke 2:25-38	
	A Light for Every Man	
	All Things Are Revealed	
	The Coming Power	
	Like the Noonday Sun	
Lesson 3	Visit of the Wise Men	July 15th
	Matthew 1:2-12	
	The Law Our Teacher	
	Take neither Scrip nor Purse	
	The Star in the East	
	The Influence of Truth	
Lesson 4	Flight Into Egypt	July 22nd
	Mathew 2:13-23	
	The Magic Word of Wage Earning	
	How Knowledge Affect the Times	
	The Awakening of the Common People	
Lesson 5	The Youth of Jesus	July 29th
	Luke2:40-52	
	Your Righteousness is as filthy Rags	
	Whatsoever Ye Search, that will Ye Find	
	The starting Point of All Men	
	Equal Division, the Lesson Taught by Jesus	
	The True Heart Never Falters	
Lesson 6	The "All is God" Doctrine	August 5th
	Luke 2:40-52	
	Three Designated Stages of Spiritual Science	
	Christ Alone Gives Freedom	
	The Great Leaders of Strikes	
Lesson 7	Missing	August 12th
Lesson 8	First Disciples of Jesus	August 19th
	John 1:36-49	
	The Meaning of Repentance	

	Erase the Instructed Mind	
	The Necessity of Rest	
	The Self-Center No Haltered Joseph	
Lesson 9	The First Miracle of Jesus	August 26th
	John 2:1-11	
	"I Myself am Heaven or Hell"	
	The Satan Jesus Recognized	
	The Rest of the People of God	
	John the Beholder of Jesus	
	The Wind of the Spirit	
Lesson 10	Jesus Cleansing the Temple	September 2nd
	John 2:13-25	
	The Secret of Fearlessness	
	Jerusalem the Symbol of Indestructible Principle	
	What is Required of the Teacher	
	The Whip of Soft Cords	
Lesson 11	Jesus and Nicodemus	September 9th
	John 3:1-16	
	Metaphysical Teaching of Jesus	
	Birth-Given Right of Equality	
	Work of the Heavenly Teacher	
Lesson 12	Jesus at Jacob's Well	September 16th
	John 4:9-26	
	The Question of the Ages	
	The Great Teacher and Healer	
	"Because I Live, Ye shall Live Also."	
	The Faith That is Needful	
Lesson 13	Daniel's Abstinence	September 23rd
	Daniel 1:8-20	
	Knowledge is Not All	
	Between the Oriental and Occidental Minds	
	The Four Servants of God	
	The Saving Power of Good	
	The Meeting-Ground of Spirit and Truth	
Lesson 14	Take With You Words	September 30th
	John 2:13-25	
Review	Healing Comes from Within	
	The Marthas and Marys of Christianity	
	The Summing up of The Golden Texts	

Fourteenth Series

October 7 – December 30, 1894

Lesson 1	Jesus At Nazareth	October 7th
Luke 4:16-30	Jesus Teaches Uprightness	
	The Pompous Claim of a Teacher	
	The Supreme One No Respecter of Persons	
	The Great Awakening	
	The Glory of God Will Come Back	
Lesson 2	The Draught of Fishes	October 14th
Luke 5:1-11	The Protestant Within Every Man	
	The Cry of Those Who Suffer	
	Where the Living Christ is Found	
Lesson 3	The Sabbath in Capernaum	October 21st
Mark 1:21-34	Why Martyrdom Has Been a Possibility	
	The Truth Inculcated in Today's Lesson	
	The Injustice of Vicarious Suffering	
	The Promise of Good Held in the Future	
Lesson 4	The Paralytic Healed	October 28th
Mark 2:1-12	System Of Religions and Philosophy	
	The Principle Of Equalization	
	The Little Rift In School Methods	
	What Self-Knowledge Will Bring	
	The Meaning Of The Story of Capernaum	
Lesson 5	Reading of Sacred Books	November 4th
Mark 2:23-38	The Interior Qualities	
Mark 2:1-4	The Indwelling God	
	Weakness Of The Flesh	
	The Unfound Spring	
Lesson 6	Spiritual Executiveness	November 11th
Mark 3:6-19	The Teaching Of The Soul	
	The Executive Powers Of The Mind	
	Vanity Of Discrimination	
	Truth Cannot Be Bought Off	
	And Christ Was Still	
	The Same Effects For Right And Wrong	
	The Unrecognized Splendor Of The Soul	

Lesson 7	Twelve Powers Of The Soul	November 18th
Luke 6:20-31	The Divine Ego in Every One	
	Spiritual Better than Material Wealth	
	The Fallacy Of Rebuke	
	Andrew, The Unchanging One	
Lesson 8	Things Not Understood Attributed to Satan	
Mark 3:22-35	True Meaning Of Hatha Yoga	November 25th
	The Superhuman Power Within Man	
	The Problem of Living and Prospering	
	Suffering Not Ordained for Good	
	The Lamb in the Midst shall Lead	
Lesson 9	Independence of Mind	December 2nd
Luke 7:24-35	He that Knoweth Himself Is Enlightened	
	The Universal Passion for Saving Souls	
	Strength From knowledge of Self	
	Effect Of Mentally Directed Blows	
Lesson 10	The Gift of Untaught wisdom	December 9th
Luke 8:4-15	The Secret Of Good Comradeship	
	The Knower That Stands in Everyone	
	Laying Down the Symbols	
	Intellect The Devil Which Misleads	
	Interpretation Of The Day's Lesson	
Lesson 11	The Divine Eye Within	December 16th
Matthew 5:5-16	Knowledge Which Prevails Over Civilization	
	The Message Heard By Matthew	
	The Note Which shatters Walls Of Flesh	
Lesson 12	Unto Us a Child I s Born	December 23rd
Luke 7:24-35	The Light That is Within	
	Significance Of The Vision of Isaiah	
	Signs of the Times	
	The New Born Story Of God	
	Immaculate Vision Impossible To None	
Lesson 13	Review	December 30th
Isaiah 9:2-7	That Which Will Be Found In The Kingdom	
	Situation Of Time And Religion Reviewed	
	Plea That Judgment May Be Righteous	
	The Souls Of All One And Changeless	

Made in the USA
Charleston, SC
23 September 2012